# the
# barefoot
# home

# the
# barefoot
# home

### dressed-down
### design for
### casual living

Marc Vassallo

The Taunton Press

Text © 2006 by Marc Vassallo
Photographs © 2006 by Ken Gutmaker,
except p. 16 © Aya Brackett, p. 17 © tarantinostudio.com,
p. 18 courtesy The MAK Center/Gerald Zugmann, p. 148 (top) © Bruce Buck
Illustrations © 2006 by The Taunton Press, Inc.

All rights reserved.

**The Taunton Press**
Inspiration for hands-on living™

The Taunton Press, Inc., 63 South Main Street, PO Box 5506, Newtown, CT 06470-5506
e-mail: tp@taunton.com

EDITORS: Katie Benoit, Peter Chapman
JACKET/COVER DESIGN: World Studio, NYC
INTERIOR DESIGN: Chris Thompson
LAYOUT: Susan Fazekas
ILLUSTRATOR: Christine Erikson, Emily Thompson (the bare feet)
PHOTOGRAPHER: Ken Gutmaker

Library of Congress Cataloging-in-Publication Data

Vassallo, Marc.
  The barefoot home : dressed-down design for casual living / Marc Vassallo ; photographs by Ken Gutmaker.
     p. cm.
  ISBN-13: 978-1-56158-807-7
  ISBN-10: 1-56158-807-5
  1.  Architecture, Domestic--Psychological aspects. 2.  Room layout (Dwellings) 3.  Interior architecture.  I. Gutmaker, Ken. II. Title.
NA7125.V37 2006
  728--dc22
                          2006002623

Printed in Singapore

10 9 8 7 6 5 4 3 2 1

The following manufacturers/names appearaing in *The Barefoot Home* are trademarks:
Boogie® board, Homasote®, IKEA®

for
Paul and Ted,
my barefoot
brothers

# acknowledgments

I want to thank everyone at The Taunton Press, especially the barefoot team of Peter Chapman, Katie Benoit, and Wendi Mijal.

I'll always be grateful to Paula Schlosser, who came up with the barefoot idea in the first place. And to Raoul Birnbaum, whose guidance and insight into my future as a writer can only now be acknowledged in a book.

A big thank you to my partner in crime, photographer Ken Gutmaker, and to his wife Linda Pope. Now if I can only win back the $2.50!

Thanks to the many architects who sent me barefoot projects to consider. Thanks to the architects whose work appears here and to the homeowners who have graciously shared their houses in this book.

Many, many thanks to my agent, Phyllis Wender.

And thanks especially to my wife, Linda, and our son, Nicky, who never fail to inspire and encourage me in our barefoot life together.

Here's to barefoot homes. Here's to barefoot dreams.

# contents

# the barefoot manifesto

## kick off your shoes. Relax. Take it easy. But don't wait until you go on vacation. Get comfortable in your everyday home.

## open up. Feel the breeze blowing through your house. Feel the warm sun on your toes, the cool tiled floor, the polished wood planks on the back deck. Pad around your uncluttered house, slipping easily from room to room. Cook and eat and live in one big space. Sleep peacefully with doors thrown open to the garden.

## embrace the sun.

Make your windows and doors really big, with lots of glass. Let sunlight pour in through clerestories, skylights, and transom windows. Curl up in a window seat, tiptoe through an open colonnade, catch the view from a sun-drenched veranda. Stretch your arms—and your house—up into the light.

## live outside as well as in.
Open whole walls to the outdoors, extend the roof outward, let the floor slip seamlessly outside to become a deck. Cook and eat on the patio, build a fire in an outdoor fireplace, take a nap in a hanging bed on the porch. Plant a kitchen garden right beside your house. Run through the wet grass to get to your backyard studio.

## adopt a barefoot state of mind.
Be glad you live in a warm climate, move to one, dream of moving to one, or act like you're in one even if you're not. Use every room in the house every day. Think informal thoughts. Simplify. Live outside when you can, bring the outside feeling inside when you can't. Never forget how good it feels to have sand between your toes.

I do not live in a barefoot home or even in a barefoot neighborhood. I live in a neocolonial house in an area of New Haven, Connecticut, called Westville. Westville has elegant homes, broad, tree-lined streets, and sidewalks wide enough for couples

# barefoot dreams

to walk hand in hand. It's the most enjoyable and edifying place I've ever lived.

And yet some of Westville's neocolonials appear a bit buttoned up. Many of these have a center hall with a grand staircase. A center hall makes a gracious entry space, but it also insinuates itself between the major rooms of the house and casts

**Relax, open up, and let the outdoors in. Create a home as open and informal as the times. Create a barefoot home.**

In the cool of an evening, light a fire outside under the stars, put up your feet, and dream a barefoot dream.
If your home isn't barefoot yet, imagine how it could be.

an air of formality about the whole main floor. These are big houses, yet the dominant type of window is a relatively small double-hung. Sometimes these modest windows are hidden behind screens and storm windows, then covered with drapes, curtains, shades, or all three. With so many layers between themselves and the outdoors, a few of my neighbors seem practically caged in their own homes!

Our house does not have a center hall, and this nod toward informality sets it on the road to bare-footedness. In our house, space flows uninterrupted between the living room, dining room, and family room through generous openings. Our backyard is

even more barefoot than the house, though it's a modest city lot. We have a kitchen garden out back, a trampoline, a basketball hoop, and a gas grill we cook on several times a week, even in winter.

We have a comfortable and relaxed house on the inside and an informal and lived-in backyard. What we don't yet have is a dynamic connection between the two.

But I have a plan. For now, since we don't have the time or the money, let's call it a dream. First we'll cantilever a translucent roof across the back of the house to create a covered area somewhere between a porch and a wide overhang. Under the roof, we'll put in five large windows across the kitchen where now there are three small ones, two French doors to the back entryway where now there is one solid door, and two more French doors in the dining room.

The bank of kitchen windows will look out on a stone patio with a wood trellis above and an outdoor fireplace. The French doors in the entryway will center on the main path through the kitchen garden. We'll build a wooden deck below the translucent roof, a step or two above the stone patio. On it we'll place a wide Indonesian teak bench, set up with a cushion and pillows like a day bed. We'll string tiny lights out to the trellis and plant wisteria so it wraps itself around the trellis posts.

Walking between the kitchen and the dining room, past the sets of French doors, will become a kind of indoor garden stroll, even in rainy or cold weather. And when warm weather arrives, we'll throw open the doors and windows and move easily from inside to outside, outside to inside, now gardening, now sipping tea on the Indonesian bench, now pausing for a cool glass of lemonade in the kitchen . . . I can almost feel it!

I have another barefoot dream, grander than the one for our New Haven home though it involves a much smaller house. My dream is to build a simple vacation home on one of the Gulf Islands in British Columbia. What I envision are three separate buildings clustered together. The main building, at the center, is built in homage to the indigenous Haida longhouses, its broad roof supported by two colossal cedar beams held aloft at each end by four thick posts carved with totem figures.

Under the roof is a single pavilion-like living area, a kitchen at one end, a hearth at the other end, and a dining area in the middle. One long side of the house faces the water. It has tall glass doors that slide apart to create an uninterrupted opening between the room inside and a terrace outside. The terrace and the floor are made of concrete, stained

**Open the doors, bring in the sun, and the difference between outside and inside falls away.**

an earthen red, and inside the floor is heated by embedded hot-water pipes, so the concrete feels warm on your feet. Large doors opposite the waterfront doors allow fresh sea breezes to blow through the space. A clerestory wraps around all four sides just below the roof, its small panes of glass letting in light from above.

On either side of the main pavilion is a bedroom building, each with its own indoor bath and outdoor shower. Sometimes I imagine a thin, glass roof connecting the buildings. Sometimes I think the only connection between the buildings should be the sky. Either way, we'll feel the salty air when we step between buildings, and the weather outside will mean something.

Perhaps you have your own barefoot dream. That's really what this book is about. Celebrating barefoot dreams others have realized and gaining inspiration to realize your own. You can take notes if you want—there's certainly much to learn—but notes are not required. In fact, at least for the first time through the book, forget pen and paper. Pour yourself a tall glass of something cool, sit back, flip off your shoes, put your feet up, and dream with your eyes wide open.

## An Informal Home for Informal Times

It's no secret our lives are less formal now than they were a hundred or even fifty years ago. Men don't wear hats to work; women don't wear gloves on the train; we don't often dine in the dining room; we don't welcome guests into a sitting parlor; most of the time we don't even come in through the front door. When we throw a party, everyone crowds into the kitchen. And we live outdoors much more than we ever did: We garden, we barbeque, we soak in the hot tub, we lounge on the deck, we leave the back door open. In all of this, our homes should offer us encouragement.

Our homes should be as informal as our lives have become. If there's a big idea behind this book, that's it. I might have called the book "Open House," had this turn of phrase not become associated with the real estate business. Simply put, that's what a barefoot home is: an open house, or, if you will, an open home. Not a home that's open on the inside only, but one that opens itself to the outdoors. A home in which inside and outside are a continuum,

**Nothing says informality like one big, open room for everyday living.**

The outdoors is more than just the space around the house; it's a place for barefoot living.

yin and yang, in constant and dynamic flux. A home that's easy to live in, easy to move through, easy to maintain. A home that's bright and airy and relaxed. A home that's open in the broadest sense. Openness. In a word, that's all there is to it. Barefootedness is a simple idea. A simple state of mind.

## Everyday home or vacation home? It hardly matters.

We expect openness and informality in a vacation home, yet many of us put up with an everyday home that is much more formal and inward-looking than we are. Imagine if your everyday home were as conducive to casual living as a vacation home. Granted, an everyday home has to accommodate certain humdrum realities, like bill paying and homework and year-round storage. So perhaps it needs a home office and a big pantry, a garage and an away room where someone can go for privacy. But beyond that, there's no reason to draw a distinction between primary residences and second homes, which is why you'll see a mix of both in this book. If anything, it's the vacation homes that have the most to teach us about how to make everyday homes more relaxed, comfortable, and delightful. I don't see why people with beach cottages and summer cabins should have all the fun.

# What makes a home barefoot?

If it isn't a spot on the beach or a perch in the mountains that makes a home barefoot, what is it? Although there's no signature barefoot style, no single way a barefoot home should look, there are some larger characteristics shared by nearly all barefoot homes. Let's take a closer look at five big barefoot characteristics, which you'll find time and again in the 23 houses profiled in this book. I've mentioned two already, informality and openness; the other three are light, texture, and an indoor–outdoor connection.

**Informality** A casual, relaxed, even laid-back atmosphere is the overarching characteristic of the barefoot home; in many ways it's the sum of the other characteristics. As a general quality, informality is hard to put your finger on, but there are aspects of informality you can point to: a bedroom with a painted wood floor; a showerhead placed right in the doorway between the bath and a private garden, so you can shower half in and half out of the house; awning windows that lift by nothing so fancy as ropes and pulleys.

**Informality is a state of mind, but a house full of casual furniture helps. And if you can't tell the living room from a porch, so much the better.**

In a barefoot home there's no need for a formal living room or dining room, just a generous, open space for sitting, eating, and hanging out.

Spend a lazy afternoon relaxing in architect Taylor Dawson's family cottage on Alabama's Lake Martin, and you'll know all about informality. The living room of this revamped cottage (shown on p. 11) used to be a wraparound porch, and it's still porch-like: open, airy, furnished with casual, wrought-iron porch chairs, a mixed bag of throw rugs, comfortable wicker rockers, even a bar fashioned from an old sailboat hull. The living room wraps around the kitchen and a dining area with funky bentwood furniture that Taylor calls "high-tech hillbilly." The spaces are connected by broad doorways, so you can slip easily into the kitchen for a second glass of lemonade and then return to your seat under a ceiling fan to while away the hours.

## Openness

The floor plan of a barefoot home is simple and open. All the spaces are used every day; there are no formal rooms set aside strictly for special occasions. There aren't that many rooms in total, little need for long hallways, hence the simplicity and compactness of the floor plans. In the typical barefoot home, as in most of the barefoot homes in this book, daily living takes place in one large space—not the imposing and often amorphous "great room" of so many suburban palaces, but a multipurpose space nonetheless, perfect for cooking, eating, and socializing.

But openness in a barefoot home is much more than a floor plan with a minimum of walls. It's the easy flow of space in three dimensions, a layering of space, an almost see-through quality. Space flows not only within the house but beyond and through the walls into the outside. Pay a visit to architect Jim Estes and his wife Darcy in their barefoot home in Rhode Island and you'll enter a tall space beneath exposed roof rafters that is at once living room, dining room, and kitchen (see the photo on the facing page). There are windows on three sides, windows up in the gable end to either side of the chimney, and five sets of sliding glass doors opening to the backyard. You're inside, and yet the room seems to stretch outward to the trees at the lawn. When a deer ambles across the backyard, you won't miss it.

Light Sunlight animates the interior of a barefoot home, accentuates its openness, and helps blur the distinction between inside and outside. In an airy, uncluttered barefoot home, light itself—falling gently on a earthen wall, filtering through a translucent roof panel, warming a concrete floor—has a quality of informality.

Welcome the sun into your home through large windows, glass doors, or skylights. Bring in light from above and even the middle of your house will shine.

The same large expanses of windows and glass doors that give a barefoot home its feeling of openness and connection to the outdoors also let in prodigious amounts of natural light. These doors and windows are often augmented by transom windows (just above the doors), clerestory windows (in the roof high above a room, as in a cathedral), or skylights, each helping to bring light deep into the

Texture is especially important in a barefoot home, where the feel of surfaces and materials contributes immeasurably to a sense of informality.

interior spaces. In a remodeled cottage in Maine, architect Will Winkelman outfitted an entire gable end with windows, then cut out a portion of the second floor to allow light from the windows to illuminate the living room below (see the photos on p. 13). Now sunlight spills down the open stairs, filters through frosted-glass balustrade panels, and bounces off the polished plywood floor, and the whole house shines from within.

In the effort to infuse your home with sunlight, you can't ignore certain obvious facts: The sun doesn't shine at night, it's cold in the winter, and sometimes there's too much sun. These must be addressed, in turn, with thoughtful attention to artificial lighting, with double-paned windows and ample insulation, and with roof overhangs, screens, and shading devices. Don't be deterred. Build the window seat that will warm your soul all year long, and when that cloudy day in December arrives, wrap yourself in blankets.

## Texture

You experience a home with all five senses, your sense of touch not the least. Even the textures that you don't actually touch affect the way

you feel. If this is true of any home, it is especially true of a barefoot home, where the pursuit of informality leads to plain materials used in an honest and straightforward manner.

In a barefoot home, you come in contact with a rich palette of textures—some hard, some soft, playing against each other in delightful ways: concrete floors, plywood panels and cabinets, polished wood trim and details, adobe and rammed earth, corrugated metal, troweled plaster walls, stone and ceramic tile.

Imagine stepping into the entry area of the Virginia farmhouse in the photo at left. You've come inside and yet the stucco walls and fieldstone floor have an outdoor air about them. The little space is flooded with light; its yellow walls feel as sunny as the day. You sit down on an old wooden stool, lay your hat beside you, and slip off your shoes. A peeled cedar column stands before you, very much like the cedars growing along the fencerow outside. A summer breeze blows through the open casements. A bee flies in and then out again. The fieldstone, tumbled and polished, feels cool and smooth on your feet.

The textures and materials in a barefoot home represent a benefit that goes beyond the pleasure of touch: ease of maintenance, an aspect so ubiquitous to barefoot homes it could be a sixth big characteristic. The appeal of easy-to-care materials is both tangible and psychological. It's tangible, of

course, because if your roof is made of sheet metal rather than asphalt, you really don't have to re-roof as often. If your walls are clear-stained plywood, you don't have to re-paint. Instead of painting you can lie in a hammock. It's psychological because knowing you have less to maintain, less to clean, less to repair and replace, you're more apt to feel relaxed and at ease yourself. It's a self-reinforcing loop, ease-of-maintenance leading to ease of living.

**A barefoot home doesn't draw a hard line between indoors and outdoors. Even when you're inside, you feel connected to the sun and the sky, perhaps to a view, and to outdoor living spaces that are just a step away.**

## Indoor–Outdoor Connection From informality and openness we come full circle to the connection between indoors and outdoors. A barefoot home puts you in touch with nature by letting the outside into the house, through views and sunlight and wide-open windows and doorways that let fresh air rush in. But the

**Though the traditional Japanese house is not necessarily informal, it always connects to the garden.**

blurring of inside and outside is not simply a matter of how big the windows are, how much glass there is; it's an attitude, always pervasive but sometimes subtle. It's stone pavers stepping seamlessly from outside to inside; it's exterior shingles on an interior wall of a master bath that feels more like a porch than a room; it's French doors thrown open, tall curtains blowing inward.

Just as important, a barefoot home literally brings you outside, with outdoor rooms—covered patios, courtyards, roof decks—and with indoor–outdoor transition spaces: porches, verandas, and loggias. The barefoot home is almost synonymous with outdoor living.

Sit around the dining table in architect Brad Burke's house in southern California (shown on p. 13) and look out the glass doors and tall windows to the patio that surrounds you. With your toes, trace the edges of the slate pavers at your feet; the same slate, in slightly rougher form, covers the patio. An outdoor fireplace at the far end of the patio seems almost to be part of the dining room. On a warm day with doors wide open, the light on the patio and in the dining room evens out, the air feels the same, and the distinction between inside and outside simply disappears.

## In search of the barefoot home

The barefoot home is a home for our time, yet, like so many things new, it's really something old made new again. I like to think that the idea of a barefoot home began with Henry David Thoreau. In a stunningly forward-thinking passage in *Walden*, written in 1854, Thoreau rails against the stuffiness and formality of the typical house of his day and imagines in its place a house that is open and informal and honest, a house "of only one room, a vast, rude, substantial, primitive hall, without ceiling or plastering, with bare rafters and purlins supporting a sort of lower heaven over one's head . . . a house which you have got into when you have opened the outside door, and the ceremony is over." In other words, a barefoot home!

## House plus garden equals home

Long before Thoreau's dream home stood the Japanese house, of all traditional houses the most barefoot by far. Even the Japanese word for *house* strikes a barefoot note, by combining the characters for house (*ka*) and garden (*tei*). A traditional Japanese house consists of one large room divided by screens that can be moved to make different arrangements of space as needed. The interior is connected to the garden by more screens, which can be slid wide open so that the garden becomes a continuation of the interior space. In the house and in the garden, a premium is placed on simplicity, emptiness, and calm. The materials used to construct the house and shape the garden are manifest and tactile: wood, paper, tamped earth, straw, bamboo, stone, water, sand. And of course when you step inside a Japanese home, you take off your shoes.

## Breaking out of the box

The Japanese house would have less to do with this book had it not inspired Frank Lloyd Wright, who developed the Prairie House toward the end of the 19th century as an antidote to the Victorian house with its boxlike rooms. Wright didn't just open the house within itself, he also opened the interior to the outdoors. "My sense of 'wall' was no longer the side of a box," Wright says in *The Natural House* in 1954. "It was enclosure of space affording protec-tion against storm or heat only when needed. But it was also to bring the outside world into the house and let the inside of the house go outside." Wright called his conceptual breakthrough "The Destruction of the Box," and architecture has never been the same since.

## Sleeping in baskets

In 1922, an associate of Wright's, the architect Rudolph M. Schindler, designed a ground-breaking house in West Hollywood, California, for himself, his wife, and another couple.

Frank Lloyd Wright's Usonian houses were decidedly barefoot. They even had heated concrete floors.

Schindler's house is the first truly barefoot home built in America. In spirit if not in style, it's the blueprint for all the barefoot houses in this book.

Schindler's house shapes itself around a courtyard with an outdoor fireplace. The living spaces have no walls on the courtyard side but huge glass doors that slide open until there's almost no distinction between the courtyard and the rooms. The materials used throughout—wood, glass, and concrete—are simple, honest, and easy to maintain.

**With its open plan and rooftop "sleeping baskets," the Schindler House was a barefoot first.**

The household members slept in the "studiorooms," as Schindler dubbed the living spaces, or on trellis-covered rooftop terraces Schindler called "sleeping baskets." Sleeping baskets! It's hard to think of anything more barefoot than that.

Unless that something is a tree. I spent my summers in a beach cottage nowhere near as thoughtfully conceived as the houses you see in this book. It wasn't a barefoot home at all. Indeed it resembled nothing so much as a chicken coop.

What it did have was a giant maple tree out in the yard. The tree was so tall and robustly leafed it created a kind of roof over our heads. Under this sylvan roof we placed a picnic table and chairs, and there we spent vast stretches of every summer day, reading, telling stories, playing cards, and, ours being an Italian family . . . eating.

There was no patio or deck under the tree, just what little grass grew without attention, and we never, ever wore shoes. In my memories of those summer days, I'm either up in the tree with my feet flat against its cool bark or I'm sitting below feeling the grass coming up between my toes. Never mind the cottage. That maple tree is my own true barefoot home.

The feel of cedar planks under your feet, sunlight filtering through a translucent roof, lunch under the trees . . . that's barefoot living.

There's nothing like sunlight to liven up a barefoot home. Sunlight casts a delirious spell, prompting us to slow down, to relax, to savor the moment. In its way, light equates with informality. But on Bainbridge Island, a short ferry ride from Seattle across Puget Sound, the sun is a steady com-

# letting the light in

panion in summer only and an infrequent guest the rest of the time. Here, a barefoot home wants all the light it can get, and yet it has to feel warm and cozy during all those dark and cloudy days.

Architect Tom Bosworth has long understood the dual need for light and shelter in the Pacific Northwest.

**A small courtyard brings light deep into the house and provides a delightful indoor–outdoor spot, sheltered from cold wind off the water, yet open to the view and sky.**

The waterfront house he designed on Bainbridge Island for Bill and Jean is all about light and openness, but it doesn't shout about them. In many quiet ways, it welcomes the sun and opens to the view, but it also offers a safe haven. For years, the house was a summer camp for Bill, Jean, their grown children, and their many grandchildren; but now it's become the couple's full-time home.

## A narrow house with views clear through

The house is long and thin, and in most places it's just one room wide. Tom imagined it as a row of camp cabins strung along the waterfront. By slicing lengthwise across the site, the narrow house lets Bill and Jean enjoy the ocean on one side and the forest on the other. There are ample windows on both sides

There's an easy flow of space from the dining room through the living room and out past the window seat. Tucked into a bay of space, the dining room also opens directly onto the waterfront porch and deck.

The house stands on the edge between the forest and the water, offering quiet views into the woods and dramatic views out to the ocean.

## what makes it barefoot

The narrow house is at its indoor–outdoor best where the hallway and courtyard doors line up. From the back porch, it's possible to **see the water** (and even the distant shore) through the hallway, the courtyard, and the front porch. The hallway and courtyard play barefoot tricks with notions of inside and out. Sitting in the courtyard, you're **open to the sky** yet you feel as if you're in a room. Walking down the hallway, you're surrounded by glass, yet you **feel as if you're strolling** down an open porch.

The long back porch serves as a covered boardwalk between the main house and the garage and guest room, making for a pleasant stroll outdoors in rain or dappled sunshine.

The waterfront deck is where summer takes place. The benches are sized just right: high enough for safety, low enough to see over from the chaise lounges, wide enough for sunbathing.

and doors everywhere, allowing the scent of cedar to waft in from the woods while salty air blows in off the ocean. But there's also protection from wind, rain, and the high summer sun. Of the house's 18 exterior doors, all but 4 open onto a porch or into a courtyard. Bill and Jean have breakfast outside on the front deck when it's warm and sunny; they sip their coffee on the porch if it's a little rainy; they sit in the courtyard if it's windy; and they sit by the big window in the kitchen when it's cold. No matter the weather, they're always connected to the land and water.

A breezeway puts some separation between the house and a guest room and office, framing a sheltered spot for sitting and a dramatic route from the back of the house to the waterfront.

# barefoot spirit

"Light is what we asked for from the first."

— *Jean*

From the waterfront deck, the courtyard (behind the opened door) appears as just another interior room, with a bit of indoor–outdoor ambiguity that adds to its charm.

▷ The open feeling of the master bedroom is both obvious and subtle. Obvious in the doors opening into the courtyard and onto the waterfront deck. Subtle in the view extending through the entire house and out the far living room window.

## Bringing light inside

Because the house stretches north to south, down the midline of the sun's path, its rooftop cupolas (properly called light monitors) act like sundials, sending down a fat beam of light in the morning, a razor-thin beam at noon, and a fat beam again in the evening. It's an intriguing way to keep track of time when the sun is out. Yet even on cloudy days, the cupolas draw light into the center of the house, where it's least expected and most welcome.

The jewel of the house is the courtyard between the master bedroom and Jean's home office nook beside the kitchen. The courtyard is open to the sky, so it won't do on rainy days, though even then it lets light into the master bedroom. But when the wind is blowing hard off the water or it's sunny out but a little cool, the courtyard is just the spot. Bill says he could sit in there all day and watch the water. He's hit on the remarkable thing about the courtyard: It's fully enclosed and yet it's entirely see-through, with a water view through the porch and a forest view through a glassed-in hallway. The courtyard is the ultimate front-to-back room in the house.

# Life on deck

There are other spots beside the courtyard that offer a sense of protection while opening up to light and views: the window seats to either side of the living room hearth; a small table in the kitchen, right up against tall windows but sheltered by the porch roof; and Jean's cozy office, dominated by a large waterfront window.

But by midsummer it's hot and dry even on Bainbridge Island, and then Bill and Jean shift their attention from the window seats and courtyard to the cedar-planked deck. When children and grandchildren visit, the deck becomes a gathering point for meals, games, and conversation. Kids jump from a raft anchored off shore, row about in a dinghy, run around barefoot. "It makes your feet hurt, just looking at it," Jean says. Perhaps. But it also warms your heart.

**Window seats to either side of the hearth are snug enough for a relaxing read yet open above and generously lit by tall windows.**

◁ **A table for two in the kitchen is a good spot on a sunny afternoon for watching boats and barefoot grand-children go by.**

## footprint

In this long, single-story house, there's a door opening out from every room, whether onto a porch, deck, breezeway, or courtyard. Though the house is essentially the width of a single room, it bumps out the additional width of the porch to create pockets of space for a piano in the living room, for the dining table, and for a sitting area in the master bedroom. The bump-outs create pockets of outdoor space as well.

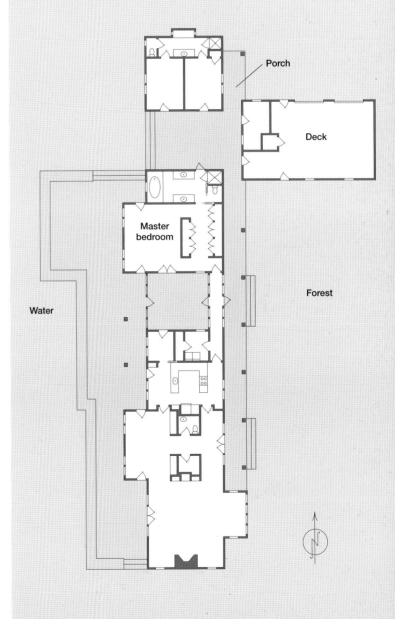

Porch

Deck

Master bedroom

Water

Forest

Architect Bob Swain loves to spend time in the mountains, yet he lives in a city neighborhood in Seattle, Washington. So he brought the mountains to his home by way of his garden. He began with a small lot—just over 43 ft. by 82 ft.—on which stood a 720-sq.-ft. ho-hum house and an equally

# house and garden are one

ho-hum 550-sq.-ft. garage/studio. The front yard was essentially a concrete driveway. Now an alpine forest begins on the sidewalk alongside the street and continues into the front yard. The concrete is gone, replaced by mountain hemlock and quaking aspen, kinnikinnick, salal, and snowberry. The sound of

With bamboo arching overhead and rough stone pavers giving way to a low cedar deck, the Asian influence on the house is unmistakable. It's easy to believe the garden is the most important room.

A long pathway of worn cedar planks and raised cedar boards leads deep into the heart of the garden before the house is revealed. Though the lot is small, there's no sense that the city is just beyond the trees.

Because the L-shaped back cabin (at right) tucks behind the front cabin (at left), the two cabins appear as one house. The shingled wall of the back cabin stops your eye, yet the basalt Buddha stone and green plants hint at the garden coming through.

water spilling into a Japanese stone basin refreshes the air.

A path of worn cedar planks crosses a garden meadow, reaches a granite stepping-stone, and turns into a raised, cedar boardwalk that leads deep into the narrow gap between the two buildings, each of which remains partially hidden in the trees. There's a barefoot trick of the mind at work. Coming down the center of the yard, focused on the basalt "Buddha stone" at the far end of the cedar path, you could be deep in the middle of the woods. Suddenly, you're inside without ever really having seen the house.

# Living in and out of two cabins

Bob's first stroke of barefoot genius was to imagine the house as an extension of his garden. His second was to resist the temptation to make a larger house by joining the two existing structures or by adding on to them. Instead, he turned each into what he calls an "urban cabin," connected only by the covered cedar boardwalk. The front cabin contains a kitchen, living room, dining area, bathroom, and guest bedroom/office. The back cabin has Bob's study and master bedroom suite. Living in the house is all about moving between the two cabins, coming into contact with the garden over and over again.

## footprint

The two "urban cabins" that make up the house sit at the back of the narrow city lot, making the most of the garden space between the house and the street as well as the length of the cedar pathway that runs down the middle of the garden. One key to the melding of house and garden is the 4-ft. 9-in. gap between the two cabins, so narrow the houses appear almost as one, yet wide enough to let the garden slip through.

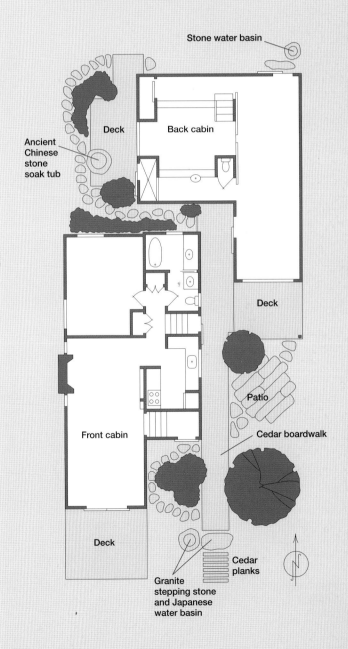

Stone water basin

Deck

Back cabin

Ancient Chinese stone soak tub

Deck

Patio

Front cabin

Cedar boardwalk

Deck

Cedar planks

Granite stepping stone and Japanese water basin

In a twist on the usual barefoot open-door policy, the patio seems close enough to touch yet lies tantalizingly beyond a window wall of fixed glass. To reach it from the study, you must step out a side door and come around.

The Buddha stone encourages a momentary pause between the two cabins that make up the house. The raised boardwalk of smooth cedar is perfect for barefooting from cabin to cabin.

▷ The rhythm of the collar ties spanning the living room ceiling is echoed in the roof-like trellis above the deck, creating a sense that the living room continues into the garden.

# Barefoot Sunday

Imagine an ideal barefoot Sunday. Bob wakes up in the back cabin to sunlight streaming through the skylights, steps down from his bed loft, and goes out to the boardwalk. He passes the basalt Buddha stone, lingers in a shaft of morning sun, then goes into the front cabin. He brews tea in the tiny kitchen and then, cup in hand, heads through the living room to the front deck, where he sits back and relaxes to the sound of wind chimes. After a morning of reading and meditating in his study, he goes outside and then in again to the kitchen, fixes a sandwich, and enjoys lunch on the stone patio surrounded by tall bamboo rustling in the wind. Later, as the sun begins to set, guests arrive down the cedar path. A buffet dinner is laid out in the kitchen, the doors are slid open, and people eat in the study, on the patio, or on the deck, moving freely in and out, fancying they're enjoying an evening in the country.

# Showering in the garden

The most striking example of Bob's indoor–outdoor lifestyle is surely the master bath, located a few steps lower than the bed loft but under the same ceiling and skylights. A more traditional bath would be a proper room, with, if nothing else, its own ceiling. In Bob's master bath, only the commode is enclosed. The bath—if you can even call it that—also serves

# barefoot spirit

"I want to sleep with the moon over my head
and take a shower outdoors every morning."

— Bob

as a passageway that leads through the shower area and out a sliding glass door to the garden. The slim master bath is as sensuous and meticulously detailed as a ship's cabin, a good fit for a scion of Cape Cod boatbuilders. And yet this warm, modern space looks out to a 700-year-old Chinese stone soaking tub. The walk-through shower is an East meets West moment, a place where Bob's Yankee heritage and Pacific Rim leanings come together, where the simple barefoot desire to take a shower in the garden every morning wins out over mere convention.

(above): The master bath opens to the garden through a sliding glass shower door. (at right): The shower head pivots for showering inside, near a fossil-filled stone wall, or outside, on the deck. A heated stone floor in the vanity area keeps bare feet toasty.

## what makes it barefoot

The bedroom area of the **master suite is on a plinth** four steps above the dressing area and the bath. The plinth puts the bed right **under the skylights** and provides room for storage underneath. Because all three areas share the same **bright ceiling,** none feels as small as it actually is. Moving from area to area under the pavilion-like ceiling is **a delightful, casual affair.**

When you boil the idea of a house down to its very essence, what you are left with is a roof over your head. A roof can't float in midair, of course, so it needs some means of support, the simplest being an arrangement of poles or posts. In all but the most exquisitely mild of climates, you also need

# barefoot under a big roof

a little protection from wind and cold, and even in paradise most of us want a little privacy, hence walls. This is all rather obvious, but it's worth bearing in mind because so many of us seem to have forgotten what a simple idea a house really is. The closer a house holds to the fundamental

If the hearth is the heart of the home, then the heart of this home lies outside under the sky, as befits a family that's gone back to the land. The house opens out to the hearth and to the whole outdoors.

The south-facing side porch extends along the full length of the house. The broad roof provides cooling shade in summer while allowing the sun to reach inside in winter.

Though the fireplace is outside at the far end of the patio, its thoughtful placement beyond an expansive wall of glass draws it into the realm of the dining area and kitchen.

notion of a roof overhead, the more likely it will be a barefoot home.

Architect Brad Burke, his wife, Honey, and their three children were living on a hemmed-in urban lot near the airport in San Diego, California—planes flying overhead, cars zooming all around, smog settling over everything—when they decided to find a quieter, healthier, more natural way to live. So Brad and

# footprint

The house has a highly ordered grid of posts holding up its roof (the black squares on the floor plan), and yet space flows freely. Under the big roof (the dotted line), rooms open to each other and to porches and patios that lie outside the walls but still within the grid. In keeping with the relaxed, open spirit of the home, spaces have been labeled on this plan as they are labeled on the architect/homeowner's floor plan—not by conventional room names but by how they're used.

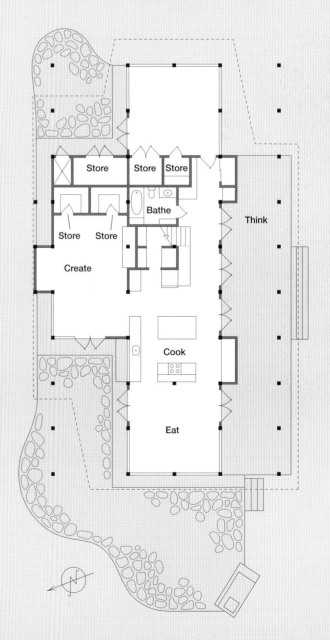

Honey headed 45 minutes north of the city, where they bought 3 acres in the foothills on which to build a house, plant a garden, and raise their children with room for them to grow. Their life is now simpler than it was in the city, but richer in outdoor experiences. Likewise, their house is smaller but more open and much more connected to the land.

# barefoot spirit

*"There are windows everywhere, so I can see what's going on all around, and I can always see the sky."*

— *Honey*

In a home that's open in all respects, there's no set use to a given space. The tables inside and out can be set up for meals or for games or for schoolwork. Which spot to choose and what to do there is up to the family . . . and the weather.

## A fresh expression of home

Brad and Honey's house is perfectly suited to their new life in the country, but it also fits in a long line of innovative houses designed and built in southern California. In particular, Brad took cues from the so-called Case Study houses designed in the postwar era by Gordon Drake, Harwell Harris, and other modernist architects. These houses tended to be sleek, flat-roofed steel-and-glass boxes, whereas Brad and Honey's house is a wood-and-glass pavilion dominated by a pitched roof with broad overhangs. Like the Case Study houses, Brad and Honey's house is composed of structural members with an infill of glass and solid panels. In keeping with their desire to live lightly on the earth, however, Brad and Honey used green building materials: composite-wood posts and beams, cement-fiber wall panels, and corrugated metal roofing.

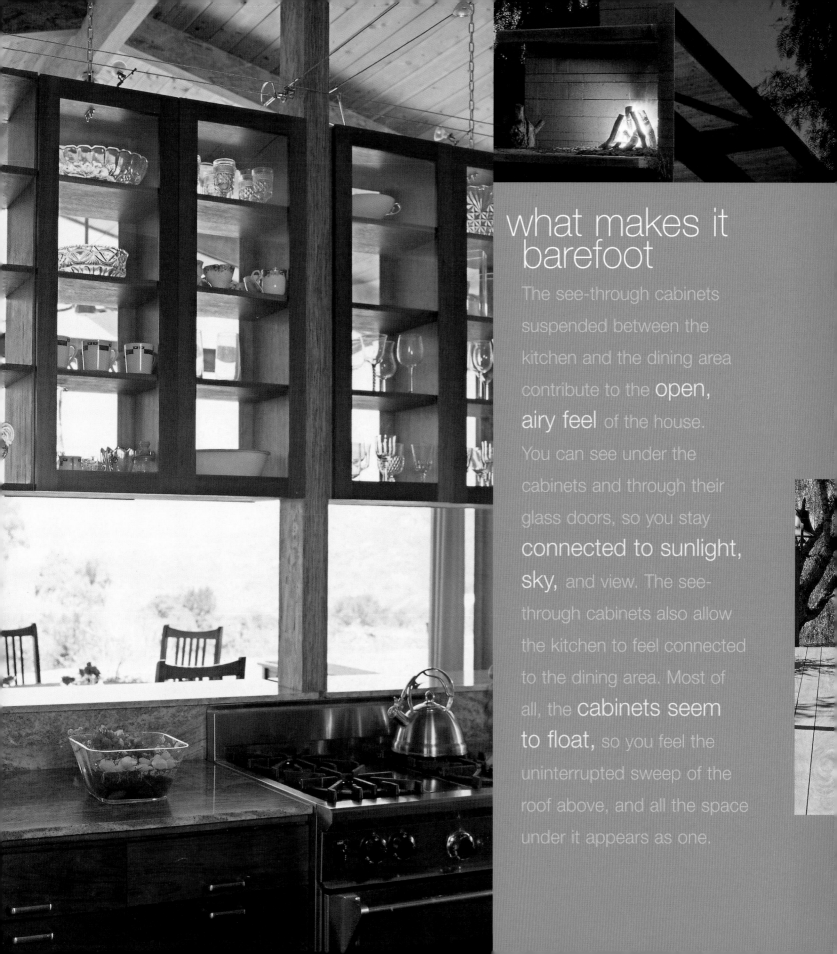

## what makes it barefoot

The see-through cabinets suspended between the kitchen and the dining area contribute to the **open, airy feel** of the house. You can see under the cabinets and through their glass doors, so you stay **connected to sunlight, sky,** and view. The see-through cabinets also allow the kitchen to feel connected to the dining area. Most of all, the **cabinets seem to float,** so you feel the uninterrupted sweep of the roof above, and all the space under it appears as one.

# Opening up inside

Under the roof, the house is open in all the obvious physical ways: There are few solid doors, spaces flow into one another, huge windows and French doors allow interior spaces to merge with porches and patio. But the house is also open in less tangible barefoot ways. On the floor plan Brad drew up, spaces aren't given conventional names but are labeled for how they're used, such as eating, cooking, and sleeping.

The bedroom is as open and relaxed as the rest of the house. Parents sleep below, surrounded by windows on three sides; children sleep in the loft above.

Think of this outdoor fireplace as being in a living room without roof or walls. Making full use of outdoor spaces enabled the house to stay small—1,500 sq. ft. for a family of five.

◁ Though the kitchen is well suited to cooking, its finely-crafted cabinetry—made from jatoba, a tropical hardwood—creates the perfect setting for lively conversation.

Extending the slate floor from the dining room to the covered patio fosters the easy flow of space from inside to outside, while giving the interior and the patio an earthy barefoot feel.

The house has no formal front door or entryway, just a path that leads past a rain chain and onto a wide side porch. To step inside from the porch, take your pick from three pairs of glass doors.

Even these labels aren't static. In all but the worst weather, the family uses the patio as its living room. They're on the patio when they sit by the fire. The kitchen is where cooking takes place, but it's also the gathering point at the center of the home, as welcome to conversation as it is to meals. Meanwhile, the space most closely resembling a living room is where the kids, who are home-schooled, do their schoolwork. The southeast-facing conservatory-like area, which had been a sitting room, is the oldest child's bedroom; the two younger children still sleep in the loft above where Brad and Honey sleep. Call it a master bedroom, if you must—but they don't.

## Putting down roots

Since moving to the foothills, Brad, Honey, and their kids have begun to put down roots, sometimes quite literally. They've tried to plant a tree a week, and their land now has scores of them, including sycamores, oaks, apples, peaches, plums, and cherries. They share the land with horses, rabbits, and chickens; and they have a pond and a large vegetable garden. Now, the really big roof the family lives under is the sky.

At night, the broad roof expresses itself as a glowing yellow sky above a home that's open and easygoing, free of clutter, and full of warmth.

In any less-than-perfect barefoot climate, living in an open house has its challenges. Consider Jamestown, Rhode Island, where winter is cold, summer is often humid and buggy, and spring and fall can be rainy and gray. Jamestown's weather isn't particularly harsh; in fact, it has a moderate

# opening up in new england

four-season climate, tempered by its closeness to the ocean. But it's not Santa Monica, California. When architect Jim Estes and his wife, Darcy, built a barefoot home in Jamestown, they had to make trade-offs.

In spite of the vagaries of southern New England weather, Jim and Darcy were determined to build

If there's a coyote crossing through the morning sunshine, he'll be seen from the master bedroom, which opens east and south into the backyard, where denizens of the woods are always welcome.

In this open interior, activity areas—such as the entry area to the left of the freestanding wall and the dining area to the right—are defined but not hemmed in. Space flows easily around the wall, toward the kitchen or down the hall to the master bedroom.

There's no back door as such. Instead, the backyard is reached through sliding doors that run the length of the house. To step in or out, you simply walk through whichever doorway is nearest.

▷ The living room is a light-filled pavilion, connected to the outdoors on three sides, cooled by cross-breezes in the summer, and warmed by a heated concrete floor in the winter.

a house that would be open, informal, and connected to the outdoors. In previous houses, they never could get guests to leave the kitchen, so in their new house, they didn't even try. The kitchen, dining, and living areas became one large space. They loved the idea of sleeping outside, so they made their bedroom feel as open as a porch. And Darcy knew she'd bring outdoor projects inside, so the house had to be casual and indestructible.

## Barefoot give-and-take

Heating a house with high ceilings and lots of windows and doors requires more energy than heating a similar house with lower ceilings and fewer openings. But rather than close in his house, Jim made it smaller. More importantly, he oriented the large windows and sliding glass doors to the south, where they'd soak up the sun in spring, fall, and winter. Jim sized the roof overhang precisely to shade the openings from the high summer sun. And he placed just a few small windows to the north, ensuring cross-ventilation in summer but protecting the house from winter winds. "You choose your battles," Jim says. "I'd rather live in a smaller space with lots of windows than in twice the space with few windows." To tilt the energy equation even more in their favor, Jim and Darcy didn't install air-conditioning. They prefer to stay connected to the outdoors and hope for a good breeze.

# barefoot spirit

*"With all the sliding doors, the whole house is a screened porch in good weather."*

*—Jim*

There's a laid-back, almost tropical quality to the living area that's in tune with barefoot living, though somewhat unexpected in the traditional New England setting.

## The pleasures of a long, thin house

A cross-breeze is a good bet in Jim and Darcy's house because it's only one room deep. Take a look at the footprint on p. 55. Remove the garage/studio wing, and the house is simply a long line of spaces: living area, dining area, kitchen, master bedroom, master bath. The utility spaces beneath the tower are naturally a bit closed off, but even their daughter's bedroom at the top of the tower is open front to back.

The master bedroom is a good example of the virtues of a single-width space. The room is divided into a bed area and a dressing area by a built-in cabinet and two columns, but these don't interrupt the flow of space and air from one side of the room to the other. All summer long, Jim and Darcy keep

The kitchen surfaces —stainless steel, concrete, and laminate— are durable, unfussy, and easy to clean, whether the project is making a quick barefoot lunch or extracting honey from the backyard hives.

## what makes it barefoot

The master bedroom has an **air of calm** and an easy connection to the outdoors. As in the rest of the house, the floor is concrete, sealed with Ashford Formula™, which causes the surface to become smoother and more polished with use. The plainness of the floor and a **lack of clutter** contribute to the room's serene atmosphere. With a cabinet behind the headboard, there aren't even night stands in the way. And because the floor is level with the ground, stepping in and out through the **wide doorway** is a breeze.

With its ample windows, fieldstone floor, and open shelves, the front entry area announces that this is a barefoot home. Though it's the main entrance, it has the rugged informality and straightforward utility of a mudroom.

▷ The house presents a quiet front to the street. A trellised entryway juts forward, welcoming visitors, but the few small windows maintain privacy. Upon entering, the openness of the house comes as a surprise.

open several awning windows high on the north wall, above a bank of built-in wardrobe cabinets. When they open the floor-to-ceiling sliding glass doors on the south side of the room, air flows past the bed and out through the north windows.

# Coming in, going out

On warm summer nights, Jim and Darcy sometimes pull their bed through the wide doorway and sleep in the backyard; easy to do because the bedroom's concrete floor is level with the ground. On sunny fall days, they keep the doors and windows open and don't worry if leaves blow in. In their barefoot home, something or someone is always coming in or going out. It might be the long rays of the winter sun, streaming through the tall south-facing windows to warm the concrete floor. It might be the two of them heading out to the backyard at night to watch a meteor shower. Or it might be Darcy bringing in honey-filled frames from her backyard hives, so she can extract the honey in the kitchen. No matter, the house is open for almost anything.

# footprint

This barefoot home affords both privacy and openness. To the north, its modest windows don't reveal too much; to the south, the entire length of the house opens to the backyard and the sun. Minus the garage/studio wing, the floor plan is simple: main living space to the west, master bedroom to the east, a small tower in the middle (with utility spaces below, bedrooms above). The entry and dining areas are shifted to align with the ruins of an old greenhouse, whose foundation walls form the edges of a long stretch of lawn.

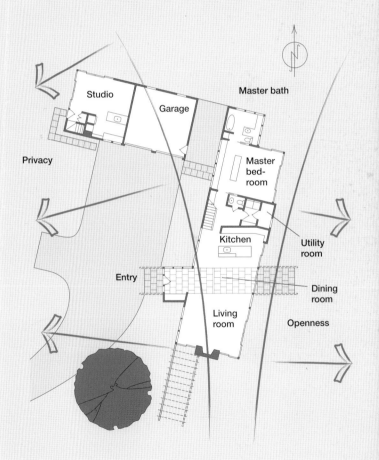

Finding an oasis in the country is easy. A couple of wooded acres down a dirt road will do, or a cabin on the riverside, or an old farmhouse out in a field somewhere. Finding a refuge in the city is a different story. If you were moving to Seattle, the last place you'd think to look would be a corner lot near a

# alfresco oasis in the city

busy street in the densely settled neighborhood known as Central City. But that's exactly where Errett and Kris and their young daughter found their own slice of barefoot serenity.

Architect Rod Novion designed the house on a lot that already had a little cottage at one end. Rod turned

The broad, translucent-paneled arbor is so high above the patio it feels like a second sky, offering a sense of shelter but letting in light and air.

In a room that's 12 ft. high, the windows have to be large to feel comfortable. These windows carry right to the ceiling, allowing sunlight to find its way deep into the space.

A barefoot blend of Queen Anne, Craftsman, and Bungalow styles, this new house feels like it's been part of the neighborhood forever. Because it looks traditional on the outside, its wide-open interior and expansive outdoor living space come as a pleasant surprise.

the cottage into a guest house that connects to the new house by a fenced courtyard. What won over Errett and Kris was the peaceful, barefoot seclusion of the house's main living space and courtyard, and especially the way these inside and outside spaces fit together.

## Barefoot bistro living

The courtyard is its own little world, sheltered by the house and hidden behind the fence and its wisteria-draped trellis. Sitting on the patio, Errett and Kris can't see other houses, and they hardly hear the traffic. Kris marvels at the transformation that takes place once they're inside the courtyard. "The sun is setting over the fence," she says, conjuring a recent moment. "It's golden everywhere, we're having wine with our friends . . . this is my idealized vision of living in a villa in Tuscany, not what you'd expect in the middle of Seattle."

Perhaps more remarkable than the courtyard and patio is the main living space, which comes as something of a surprise upon stepping through the foyer into the house. The space is 12 ft. high and completely open, its kitchen area, dining area, and two sitting areas defined by a single column and the area's L shape, which gives the sitting area by the hearth a bit of separation. The space isn't grand, however, so much as it is generous. It calls to mind a warm and comfortable bistro more than a living room, which seems entirely appropriate for a barefoot city home.

From the open-air kitchen (in the background), it's one barefoot step to the island countertop, two more to the dining table, three more to the patio. Bright, brighter, brightest.

# barefoot spirit

"This is my idealized vision of living in a villa in Tuscany,
not what you'd expect in the middle of the city !"

— *Kris*

The living space opens fully on two sides onto a covered patio that itself could be a quiet outdoor café. The easy flow between the main space inside and the patio outside is what makes the house so delightful, whether Errett and Kris are entertaining guests or relaxing while a cool breeze comes through the French doors.

## Height equals light

Rod made the main living area tall to bring as much natural light into the space as possible. The 12-ft.-high ceilings allow room for clerestory windows high above the kitchen cabinets, where their translucent glass captures sunlight slanting past the neighbor's house and diffuses it throughout the space. The high ceiling also allows for transom windows above the French doors and—most important of all—sets the roof of the arbor at the same lofty height. It's the unusually high arbor roof that gives the whole courtyard its delightfully buoyant atmosphere, adding to the feeling of seclusion, sheltering the patio during the inevitable Seattle rains, yet welcoming in every last drop of sunshine.

With the house tucked to one side of the lot, the fenced courtyard stretches nearly the full length of the property, increasing its feeling of expansiveness.

## what makes it barefoot

The transom windows above the French doors are essential to the indoor–outdoor feel of the main living space. Without them, light filtering through the translucent roof of the patio wouldn't reach as far inside as it does. More significant, the transom windows allow you to see the translucent roof from well back in the space and to read it as a continuation of the ceiling high above you.

Fan and Don's cottage on Martha's Vineyard is exactly what it appears to be: a set of three cedar-clad, drywall-lined boxes. What's missing in terms of color and detail appears in vivid relief each morning when the huge glass doors of the living room are opened to a green lawn, a riot of wildflowers, a

# barefoot cubed

sliver of blue ocean, and a burst of fresh air. A dirt path cuts through the tall grass edging the lawn, heading north toward the unseen shore, a tantalizing invitation to wander. The living room may be a simple, unadorned space, but one of its walls is a 10-ft. by 24-ft. landscape painting, and whenever

The cottage is a simple, low-slung affair that harkens back to island camps of old. Here the land is what matters most. And because the cottage is divided into three buildings, outdoor living is ensured.

Two huge doors roll back to draw the land and the ocean (which is felt even when unseen) into the living space of the center cabin.

Fan and Don wish, they can jump into the canvas and become part of it.

# Fish camp fundamental

Fan and Don were already living year-round on Martha's Vineyard, an island off the coast of Massachusetts, when they bought a plot of land on a windswept hillside near their main home as a getaway spot, "a getaway from a getaway," as Fan says. What they yearned for was a fish camp, or at least a modest little house with the primitive feel of the fish camps once common on the island, basic cabins that took a backseat to the outdoors. They wanted a place where they could go to a garden or just relax, where Fan could write poetry and paint, where family and friends could stay or island visitors could rent by the week.

Architect Charles Rose had worked with Fan and Don on their year-round house, and he was their choice for the new getaway as well. After studying the lay of the land to find the view, Charles created a barefoot camp composed of three small cabins. The main cabin in the center has one large room with a kitchen area, dining and sitting areas, and a half bath. To either side are bedroom cabins.

The cabins are elementally simple, clad in weathered gray shingles, like traditional island cottages, but with gently sloped shed roofs, not cottage-like

The long bedroom cabin (at left) and the cabin at the center form two sides of a grassy terrace with a hint of the ocean beyond. The terrace can be a place for quiet contemplation, as it is here, or the scene of a full-blown lobster fest.

The kitchen is as simple as can be, just a straight run of cabinets and a corner open to southern light and a green view. In place of upper cabinets, large windows tilt open unexpectedly from the bottom.

# barefoot spirit

*"I want my guests to say, 'I think I'll go up to the roof deck and say good night to the stars'."*

*— Fan*

If ever there was an argument for a flat roof over the traditional pitched one, the deck on top of the center building would be it. Where the steel railing touches down lightly upon it, the deck feels like a platform hovering in midair, an outdoor room in its purest form.

The outdoor staircase takes you on a little journey, away from the ocean toward the bedroom cabin, then across the bridge, looking west over the deck and the land, and finally onto the deck, where, with a turn, the ocean reappears as if by magic.

pitched roofs. The spaces inside are delightfully spare; but what really matters are the courtyard-like outdoor areas formed by the buildings, the energetic gaps between the cabins, and especially the roof deck on top of the center cabin, with its sweeping island view.

## Outdoor education

If you stay at Fan and Don's cottage, you'll get a complete lesson in barefoot living. No matter where you begin the morning, you learn that you can never really live *in* the cabins without also living *out* of them. It's what comes of making a house in three parts, a lesson in barefoot geometry that you won't soon forget.

Perhaps you wake up in one of two bedrooms in the cabin to the west. You see a slice of water just as you rise, and soon you're out the screen door. With a spring in your step, you touch down on a granite stone, turn and see the ocean again, this time in the gap between the buildings, and then you walk across the grass and under a ship-like metal bridge to another stepping-stone and into the sun-filled center cabin.

The steel footbridge serves triple duty: providing a way to reach the roof deck, visually linking the west building with the center building, and framing a view toward the ocean.

# footprint

This simple island cottage is made up of three cabins: a living/dining/kitchen cabin at the center and a bedroom cabin to either side. The outdoor terraces suggested by the cabins are as important as the spaces inside, and the slots of space between the cabins are most important of all. It's by moving through these gaps that you fully experience the ever-changing character of the land, the ocean views, and the three-piece cottage.

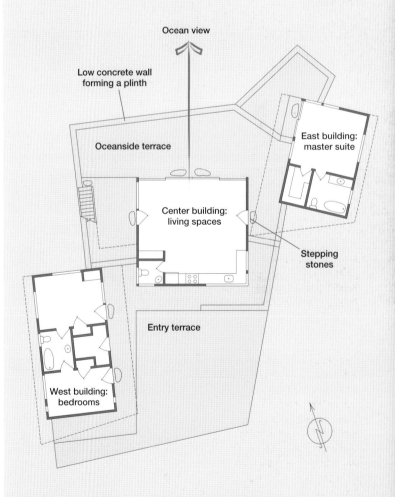

Ocean view

Low concrete wall forming a plinth

Oceanside terrace

East building: master suite

Center building: living spaces

Stepping stones

Entry terrace

West building: bedrooms

The differences between inside and out, one building and the next seem insignificant when everything is bathed in the same early morning light.

Half-hidden in the late-afternoon light, the taut steel bridge to the roof deck is infinitely more barefoot and alluring than a clunky indoor staircase could ever be.

If you wake up in the bedroom in the cabin to the east, you take a similar stroll, heading away from the ocean under a canted roof overhang. Just as you turn to step into the center cabin, the low sun catches the back of your legs.

If you're lucky to have spent the night on the roof deck, snug in a sleeping bag while the stars and the moon travel across the sky, you'll be up early to see the dark blue ocean stretching north, soft light falling on a distant shore, and you'll thank Fan and Don for building simply and being willing to share.

## what makes it barefoot

The view from the rooftop offers an entirely fresh perspective on the house, the **land,** and the **ocean.** The deck feels like an outdoor room, with four short walls and the sky for a ceiling, the perfect spot for **relaxing,** reading, dining, or sleeping **under the stars.** Behind the romance are two **small details** that make it work: a slightly sloped waterproof roofing membrane under the wood decking that channels rainwater into downspouts, and an electrical outlet, **thoughtfully placed** on one of the parapet walls.

In a barefoot home, openness expresses itself in two dimensions—outward into the land, and upward toward the sun and sky. Openness is also an attitude—a willingness to relax, get comfortable, come together inside, and extend home life into the outdoors. Sometimes a house conspires against this, whether

# building upward
## and outward

it's oriented poorly to the sun or it lacks a connection to the yard, and the time comes to make a change.

Jon and Shannon, who live in Cardiff, California, a quiet beach town north of San Diego, had a modest, single-story cottage with two bedrooms and a bath.

Unlike a more traditional home, this barefoot home isn't afraid to open up in front. Visitors enter a hall that spills right into the dining room and kitchen. The dining room, in turn, opens through floor-to-ceiling windows and French doors onto a front-yard patio.

# barefoot spirit

"Almost every night we have wine on the deck while the little kids play and watch the sun go down."

—Jon

The house shape takes full advantage of barefoot opportunities. The two-story section captures an ocean view, as does the trellis-covered roof deck. The one-story section extends the main living space into the garden.

▷ Although the kitchen is tidy and efficient, it doesn't feel cramped because it opens into the dining room (at left) and has an over-the-counter view into the living room (at right). The door to the side yard is the quickest route to the outdoor barbecue grill.

Though the cottage was five blocks from the ocean, it didn't have a view. Jon had the good fortune of working from home, but he was stuck in the converted garage. The cottage had its charms, but it was falling apart; and as the family grew from one child to three, the home became increasingly cramped. Realizing something had to give, Jon and Shannon turned to their close friends and neighbors architects Taal Safdie and Ricardo Rabines.

## Reaching for a view, connecting to the garden

After much back and forth, Jon and Shannon decided that the only option was to tear down their cottage and rebuild from scratch. Taal and Ricardo designed a new house in two sections: one with living space below and an open roof deck above, and the other with children's bedrooms below and the master suite and Jon's home office above. The one-story section extends into the garden; the two-story section rises to capture the view.

The heart of the house is the nearly open living space that extends from the front yard to the backyard. At the center is the kitchen, which opens across an island counter to the dining room and

The sitting area in front of the fireplace inside and the table on the patio feel like two spots within a single living space, extending from the chimney out to the edge of the patio.

The living room isn't large, but it opens out to a brick patio and the backyard garden. With doors hiding behind the curtains and the wood floor level with the brick pavers, the indoor–outdoor connection feels especially smooth.

connects via a pass-through to the living room. The dining room is toward the front, and the living room toward the back. This decidedly barefoot arrangement of rooms flip-flops the old standard of public space to the street, private space in back. Visitors step almost immediately into the dining room and kitchen, while the family makes everyday use of the living room and its garden connection.

The master bedroom on the second floor has a huge ocean-facing corner window that gives the couple the feeling of waking up on a sailboat. An avid surfer, Jon also has an ocean view from the corner desk in his second-floor office. Now he watches the waves, and when the surf's up, he takes a break from work and heads for the ocean. The master bedroom and office open onto a roof deck with an even more sweeping view. The family spends its evenings on the deck, where they light a fire in the brick fireplace on cool nights.

**The large roof deck offers a view of the Pacific Ocean that draws the whole family outside every evening to watch the sun go down.**

## footprint

The house is composed of two sections: a single-story section with the living room, kitchen, and dining room below and a large deck above, facing the ocean view; and a two-story section with children's bedrooms below and a master suite and home office above, opening out to the deck. The two sections are divided by a hallway that runs the length of the house, connecting the front yard and backyard gardens.

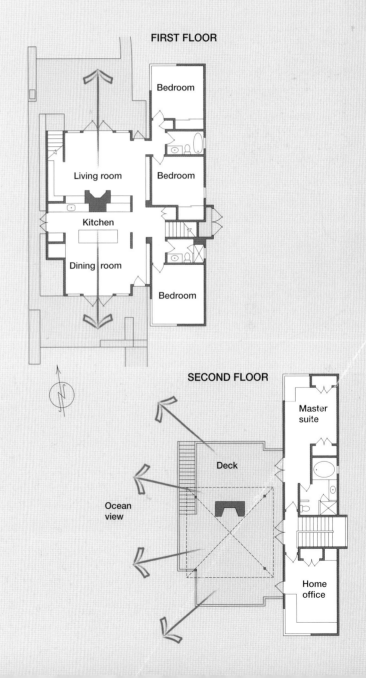

**FIRST FLOOR**

Bedroom

Living room

Bedroom

Kitchen

Dining room

Bedroom

**SECOND FLOOR**

Master suite

Deck

Ocean view

Home office

The trellis over the roof deck provides visual interest and a secure feeling of shelter while maintaining a sense of openness.

An open staircase, brightly lit from the glass doors above, leads to a roof deck with a large ocean view. The stairs provide a moment of anticipation, making the view that much more dramatic when it appears.

# Keeping it warm

The new house balances the openness Jon and Shannon wanted with the warmth and intimacy of their old cottage. The warmth comes from the use of natural materials throughout: clear cedar for the siding, brick for the hallway floor and for the patios and outdoor stairs, fir for the ceilings and beams, and reclaimed eucalyptus for the floors. The eucalyptus flooring has nail holes and signs of age that lend the house a lived-in feel.

The house has another kind of warmth, and Taal and Ricardo feel it every time they come over for a visit. Teenage kids hang out on the deck upstairs, grown-ups sit and talk in the living room and dining room, little kids ramble down the hall and out into the backyard, and Jon and Shannon take it all in from the kitchen. In this barefoot house, there's room for everyone.

## what makes it barefoot

The house has four large **corner windows:** two downstairs in the children's bedrooms and two upstairs—one in the master bedroom, one in the home office. The windows are frameless at the very corners, where two glass panes are mitered seamlessly together. The glass corner creates a **see-through effect** that echoes the house's overall indoor–outdoor character. From inside, the corner windows break down the boxiness of the rooms and **draw in the view.**

Nothing is worse than a vacation house that's just as complicated and cut off from the outdoors as so many year-round houses have become. How can you get away from it all if you bring it all with you? How can you get closer to nature — which might be the reason to stay at the beach or in the

## open to the breeze

mountains — if you block it out with air-conditioning, television, and carpeted rooms with little windows? Along the shores of Lake Martin an hour north of Montgomery, Alabama, people have taken to build-ing second homes with all the amenities. It's under-standable and perhaps inevitable, but it isn't for

It's possible to run barefoot in a straight line from the porch to the end of the dock and off the dock into the lake. The thrown-open door invites just such a course of action.

Handmade signs on a dirt road near the lake make it known that the cabin is in a barefoot neighborhood.

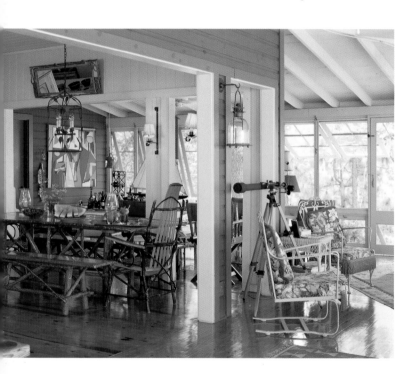

The dining area, in what had been an enclosed living room, is now seamlessly connected to the wraparound porch. Where there were once doors and windows, now there are just wide openings.

Martha Jane and husband M.T. "Most people around here want air-conditioning, but that's not how we think," says their son, architect Taylor Dawson III, the designer in the family. Taylor orchestrated a remodeling and upgrading of the cabin his parents built some 30 years ago, determined to keep the barefoot spirit of the original, which was, as he puts it, "one step ahead of camping out."

## Just a big old screened porch

The cabin stands at the end of a 10-mile-long dirt road, on a south-facing spit of land surrounded by water on three sides. The family calls the place Land's End. When M.T. first built it, it had a back-of-beyond quality to it, with exposed framing, no insulation, and a pantry stocked with dishes and glasses given away by the local gas station with a fill-up. There were two tiny bedrooms, a tight kitchen, a bath, and a small living room. The essence of the cabin was a 12-ft.-wide screened porch that wrapped around three sides of the living room, each side facing the water. The family lived on the porch, and Taylor and his three sisters slept out there every night. When they came in from sailing, they'd hang wet sails to dry on the porch rafters.

Taylor has fond memories of the porch draped with billowy sails. But times change, families grow, and with the arrival of grandchildren, Martha Jane and M.T. decided the cabin needed to grow a little, too.

With the lights on at dusk, the cabin reveals itself to be a wide porch wrapped around a kitchen and dining area. It's hard to tell where the porch ends and the rooms begin, and that's precisely the point.

# barefoot spirit

"There's really no schedule. Whatever people feel like doing, they do."

*—Taylor*

Open to lake breezes on three sides, sheltered under a high roof, and cooled by air drawn into its cupola, the dogtrot is the place to be when it's hotter than blazes outside.

The entryway to the dogtrot signals the playfulness of the house with a sailboat cut-out; metal sconces shaped like large-mouth bass; and, looking exotic but not out of place in this Alabama lake cabin, a kilim carpet.

## Adding on without closing in

Taylor's goal in remodeling was to add space without spoiling the simplicity and openness of the original cabin. He decided to clip two bedrooms and baths to the front of the cabin by way of a covered but otherwise open area, known as a dogtrot. The dogtrot has a cupola on top that draws air up through it like a chimney. The ceilings in the dogtrot and bedrooms have exposed rafters, an echo of the porch ceiling, though in places there's paneling cut in a curve, a reminder of the drying sails of old. The dogtrot is meant to be a place for working on boats, but Taylor admits what actually goes on in its cool shade is a lot of "rocking and relaxing."

It used to be that when it rained, everything on the porch got wet. To make the porch more weatherproof without diminishing its essential porchness, Taylor kept the screens but added ingenious flip-up windows between each framing stud, some 32 window sashes in all. The windows are raised with ropes attached to pulleys hung from struts extending

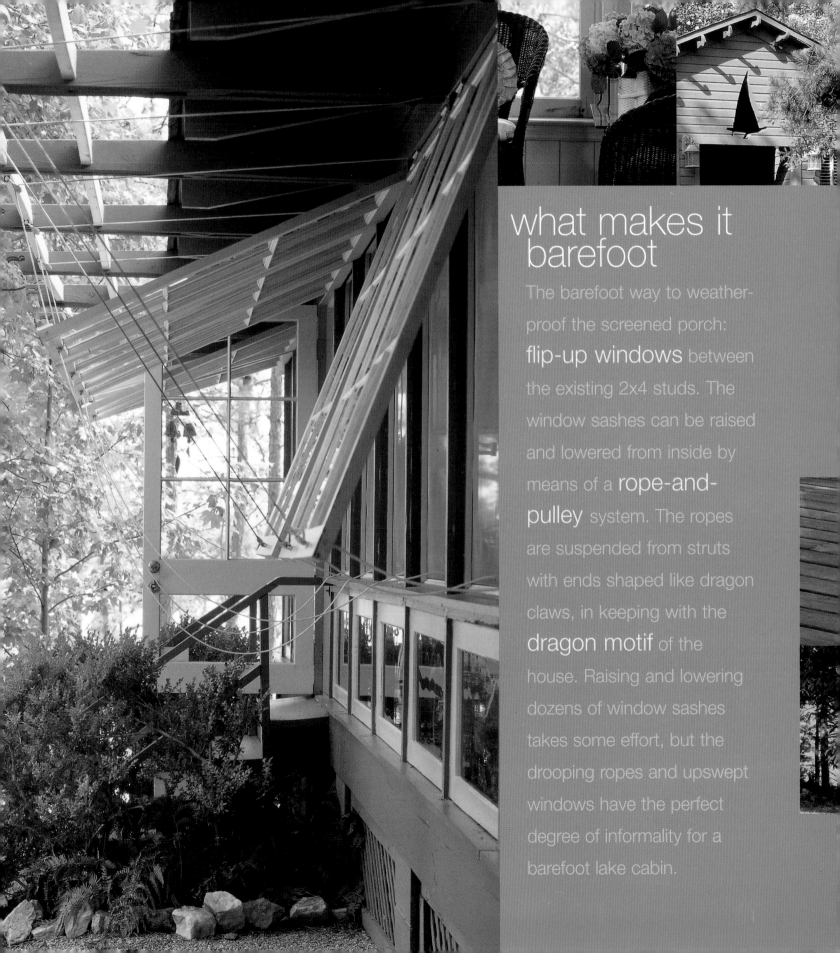

## what makes it barefoot

The barefoot way to weather-proof the screened porch: **flip-up windows** between the existing 2x4 studs. The window sashes can be raised and lowered from inside by means of a **rope-and-pulley** system. The ropes are suspended from struts with ends shaped like dragon claws, in keeping with the **dragon motif** of the house. Raising and lowering dozens of window sashes takes some effort, but the drooping ropes and upswept windows have the perfect degree of informality for a barefoot lake cabin.

The cabin and its secluded point are called Land's End. In homage to the ancient mapmakers who drew dragons beyond land's end to warn sailors of unknown dangers, dragons form a whimsical motif here on the dock and in the cabin as well.

In place of central air-conditioning, the cabin at Land's End offers a shaded dockside seat and the cool waters of vast Lake Martin.

In keeping with the easy-going barefoot spirit of the porch, a favorite old sailboat finds new life as a bar.

Each of the new bedrooms is a small version of the porch, with flip-up windows, exposed ceiling framing, and a porch-like air of openness.

The mellow green color of the cabin helps it blend with its surroundings and keeps it looking humble. Many neighboring lake houses are painted the same color, known locally as "Buddy Green," a barefoot color if there ever was one.

from the eaves. They're lowered with a second set of ropes running through little holes in the screens. The ropes are tied off to metal cleats, just like rigging on a sailboat. With the porch windows flipped up, the cabin remains open to the breezes.

## Barefoot days of summer

To hear Taylor describe it, a weekend at Land's End is every bit as laid-back as the cabin itself. Breakfast might be at 10 in the morning, taken on the porch,

with coffee sipped outside on the deck. Then it's "get on the lake time." They fish, they sail, they swim, they try to stay cool. "Soaking in the water," Taylor says, "that's our air-conditioner." Late in the afternoon, someone gets up the energy to make sandwiches for lunch. Then it gets even hotter, and people take naps. As the day winds down, everyone congregates on the deck and watches the sun set across the lake. Dinner might not happen until 10 or 11 at night. "There's really no schedule," Taylor says. "Whatever people feel like doing, they do."

# footprint

Even with the addition of two bedrooms and an open-air dogtrot (the shaded area on the plan), this Alabama lake house is dominated by a wraparound screened porch with views to the water on three sides. The living room opens fully to the porch, making the entire lakeside half of the house one big space for hanging out and keeping cool.

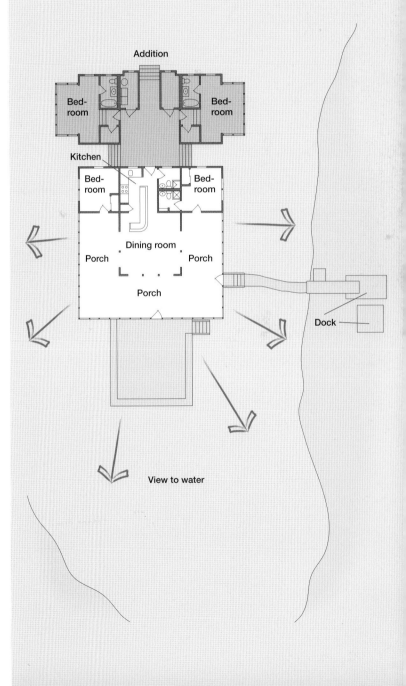

If there's a quintessential barefoot floor plan, this is it: a single, large, open space for cooking, eating, and socializing, surrounded by small spaces for sleeping, bathing, welcoming guests, or enjoying a quiet moment. Regardless of the particulars, this general arrangement allows family members and

# a plan for coming together

friends to come together in the main living space, yet go their separate ways when they need a break. With one big space for the bulk of day-to-day living, openness and informality are nearly ensured. The 1,860-sq.-ft. strawbale house designed by architects David Arkin and Anni Tilt for a rare open spot

This strawbale home opens up to the outdoors and welcomes guests in its embrace. You might find yourself pulling up a chair on the patio before ever going inside.

A model of barefoot simplicity, the storage wall running the length of the house is nothing fancier than the necessary wall framing, ordinary lumber turned into shelving.

The lower, sloped ceiling lends intimacy to the kitchen and dining areas within the main living space, while the tall peak offers light and breathing room.

▷ Clerestory windows in the high walls of the main living space draw light deep into the house and ventilate the house on warm days. Gazing through the high windows, you can track the sun or watch the clouds go by.

in densely populated Mill Valley, California, represents the barefoot footprint in its pure form; there aren't even any hallways to muck it up.

When Ren and Rachel bought the house, they became the beneficiaries of an unlikely rural retreat— an earth-friendly strawbale home tucked away in a meadow behind a cul-de-sac of ordinary suburban houses. Slipping down the long driveway between the neighboring houses, passing through the farm gate, and entering the pasture is like a trip to the country, though San Francisco lies just across nearby Golden Gate Bridge.

# A barefoot house of straw

David and Anni honored the rural character of the land by placing the house to one side of the property, leaving the meadow largely intact, and by drawing inspiration from the simplicity and directness of vernacular farm buildings. In an entirely pleasant and appropriate way, this strawbale house has the airy, open quality of a barn. It isn't as spare or as rough as a barn, of course, but it is as purposeful. Everything is there that needs to be there—and nothing more. This straightforward approach results in a deeply restful atmosphere that's especially appealing to Ren, who spent several years in Japan with his family, where he learned to appreciate the beauty of living simply.

# barefoot spirit

"With an outdoor fireplace, having friends over is a bit like going camping."

— *Ren*

The thick storage wall adds a degree of separation between the main living space and the bedrooms. Its depth echoes that of the bed alcove in the strawbale wall beyond.

The front entry functions like a traditional Japanese *genkan,* the entry space where shoes are removed. But unlike in a formal *genkan,* the atmosphere here is as laid-back as a mudroom.

The house also reflects farm buildings in its materials: corrugated metal roofing, concrete floors, galvanized stovepipes, barn-style sliding doors, and of course the strawbales that make up the exterior walls. Strawbales are a great barefoot building material because they give a home depth and texture. They're natural; imperfect; and, well, fat. "You can do anything with strawbales except have skinny walls," Anni says. In this house, every opening in the thick strawbale walls is a mini-room that extends interior space into the landscape. It's a subtle effect, an additional 2 ft. here and there, but it has real impact. In the kitchen, the sink counter fits within the depth of the wall, pulling you closer to the pasture. In the bedrooms, the deep window jambs become cozy bed alcoves that put you literally in touch with the earthen walls as they inch you outward.

## Good for the earth, good for the soul

For all their barefoot texture, the strawbale walls were chosen because they're easy on the earth. Strawbales are an inexpensive, renewable, natural material that add strength, sound-dampening qualities, and a high degree of insulation to the walls. In Ren and Rachel's house, the bales are wrapped with wire mesh and covered with 2 in. to 3 in. of a

## what makes it barefoot

An **outdoor hearth** creates a focal point and gathering spot, and fire has an **elemental allure.** This fireplace shares a chimney with the indoor fireplace, allowing you to enjoy the barefoot feeling of huddling against the **warmth of the house** with the **cool night** to your back.

The corner living area gains barefoot character from a trio of richly textured materials: a peeled eucalyptus column, an earthen-walled hearth, and pressed ryegrass ceiling panels.

▷ The placement of the house at the edge of the property preserves the meadow as a generous outdoor space.

sprayed-on, stabilized earth that give them the richness and warmth of terra-cotta. Most of the other materials used to build the house are equally green. In a refrain to the straw embedded in the walls, the ceilings are covered with panels made from pressed ryegrass. To save on wood, the clapboard siding planks are made from a combination of cellulose fiber and cement. Concrete floors hold heat from the sun and warm the house on cloudy days by radiating heat from embedded hot-water pipes. Ren says he can feel the warmth coming up into his toes.

What's good for the earth, it turns out, is good for barefoot living. On cool nights, Ren likes to lie on the warm concrete inside and gaze through the clerestory windows as fog rolls in over the house. When he and Rachel have friends over, he says, "It's a little bit like going camping. We lie by the fire, the doors are open, people come in and out." There are no firm lines drawn between one area of the room and another, or between indoors and outdoors. That's the point of the big space, after all, bringing everything and everyone together.

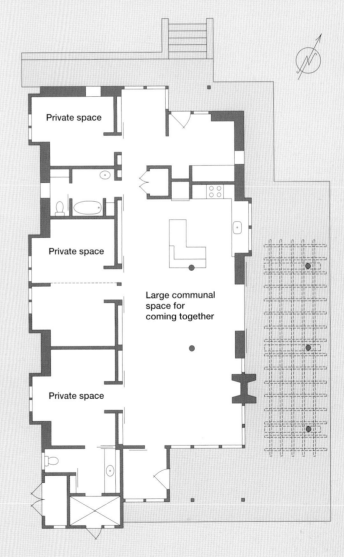

## footprint

The everyday life of the house happens in one big, barefoot living space. This main space is 18 ft. wide by 38 ft. long, or 684 sq. ft.—large enough to feel generous, small enough to feel comfortable. Surrounding the main living area, and protecting it from the harsher conditions of north and west exposure, are compact private spaces. These rooms are no larger than they need to be, which encourages full use of the main living space.

Private space

Private space

Private space

Large communal space for coming together

One of the best recipes for creating an indoor–outdoor feeling in a barefoot home is to use materials typically thought of as exterior materials —cedar shingles, stone, weathered wood—on the inside of the house. Add traditional exterior colors —browns and greens, for instance—combined

# farmhouse on the beach

with large windows and generous door openings, and suddenly you're in the dining room but you feel as if you're on the porch, enjoying an alfresco meal. That's exactly the feeling Craig gets in the dining room of the waterfront vacation cottage he shares with Lisa and their young daughter.

The cottage is perched on a narrow bank above Hood Canal. Following the lay of the land, the rooms inside step down from the entry hall to the porch, parallel to the water; the terraces continue stepping down to the rocky shore.

# barefoot spirit

"I want guests to feel comfortable walking in
with wet shoes or going barefoot."

— *Craig*

When Craig asked architects Bob Hull and Scott Wolf to design a hideaway on Hood Canal, a narrow stretch of seawater on Washington State's Olympic Peninsula, he hadn't envisioned the inside–outside dining room, but he knew he wanted a casual, comfortable retreat for unwinding from his busy work life in Seattle. His clipping file was filled with images of New England saltboxes, painted wood, and wide porches . . . seemingly at odds with his desire for a cottage in tune with its Pacific Northwest surroundings. Craig called the feeling he was after a "beach farmhouse." It would be Bob and Scott's job to pull together the notions of beach and farmhouse and fit them both into a small cottage on a challengingly steep and narrow site.

## Following the lay of the land

A steep gravel drive leads down to a turnaround between the cottage and a boathouse, which has an airy guest bedroom on its second floor, close enough to the cottage but with a measure of privacy. From the turnaround, the cottage entry is through a two-story stair hall that Bob calls "captured space" because it feels like outdoor space with a roof over it. From the hall and the adjacent kitchen, the interior spaces step down to the shore, parallel to the water.

In the entry hall, space flows like a river, slipping under the bridge between the bedrooms and down past the stone chimney to the living room.

◁ The entry hall blurs the lines between inside and out. The shingled wall by the stairs looks like an exterior surface; the reclaimed pine flooring is as unfussy as porch decking; and the ceiling continues outside, beyond the tall transom window above the door.

From the kitchen, it's three steps down to the dining room, then three more down to the living room. Beyond the living room, the porch steps down to a stone patio, then to a lower patio, and on down to the water's edge, where Craig and Lisa sit in the morning to read the paper.

The terracing of the rooms puts a lot of visual emphasis on the floors and stairs. On top of that, Craig wanted his guests to feel comfortable about going barefoot or walking in from the beach with wet shoes. The all-important flooring had to be handsome, unfussy, and hard wearing. Craig chose reclaimed antique heart-pine boards with a lifetime of nicks and scratches already in them. Washed a weathered gray, the wide boards feel as smooth and gently worn as driftwood.

## Barefoot sweet spot

The dining room is the sweet spot. On its uphill side, a wall of windows rises to reveal a green cascade of trees and plants. The massive trunk of an ancient fir tree stands just outside, as though behind the glass of a giant terrarium. On the opposite side, four glass doors fold out of the way to open the dining room onto a narrow deck above the water. The illusion of being outside is heightened by the kitchen wall, which from the dining room looks like a shingled house front, its pass-through window and open

**Though the living room is quite small, its windows and doors are generously sized, a shift in scale that results in an easy barefoot openness, a sense that the room continues out to the porch columns.**

▷ **The dining room is an indoor space that feels like an outdoor porch. This indoor–outdoor feeling is created by the cedar-shingled kitchen wall and by huge glass doors that open fully to a deck above the water.**

The boathouse (left) is the perfect place for guest quarters, with a glimpse of the main house from the bath (facing page) and a tall double-window that looks like a doorway but leads only to the view (below). Cable railings keep the large opening safe without spoiling its airy effect.

doorway framed as though they were on the exterior. Even the soapstone top of the buffet contributes to the indoor–outdoor effect. With the doors peeled back and the morning sun streaming in, the airy dining room feels like a wide porch off the kitchen, hovering above the water.

# Life is an oyster

In the end, Craig got the beachy farmhouse he wanted, a place not so very different in barefoot appeal from the tents he pitched in the summer as a young boy, just up the road, where his parents still

## footprint

The cottage was conceived of as two smaller houses, one with the living room below and master bedroom above, the other with the kitchen below and a child's bedroom above. The dining room, entry/stair hall, and master bath occupy the space between the two houses. These in-between spaces have floor-to-ceiling glass; exterior materials, like cedar shingles, on their surfaces; and a strong sense of openness and flow. Walking through these spaces from the bedrooms to the kitchen or from the kitchen to the living room feels a lot like stepping outside and back in again.

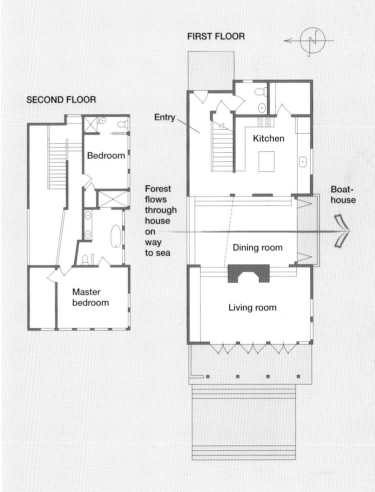

FIRST FLOOR

SECOND FLOOR

Entry

Kitchen

Bedroom

Forest flows through house on way to sea

Boat-house

Dining room

Master bedroom

Living room

Standing under this minimalist outdoor shower feels like bathing under rainwater that's splashing down the lush hillside.

Tucked between the forest and the shore, the house has the diminutive scale and simple lines of an old waterman's cottage combined with the oversize windows and doors of a contemporary barefoot home.

have a cabin. His own cottage is open to frequent visits from family and friends. Days are spent on the water and on the beach, drinks kept cool in the boathouse, which becomes a cabana when the barn doors at each end are slid open. Craig sets crab traps offshore, hauls in a couple dozen big Dungeness, grills them on the patio, and tosses the shells back in the water. And if the crabs are hiding, there are Hamma Hamma oysters waiting right on the rock-strewn beach.

## what makes it barefoot

A cedar-shingled wall, painted ceiling boards, and a claw-foot tub plunked down by the **oversize windows** lend the second-floor master bath the casual air of having been **shaped over time.** The room feels as if it could have been an outdoor porch that was enclosed as a sunroom and later converted into a bath. Muted colors, clean lines, **light pouring in . . .** the simple pleasure of bathing outdoors has been brought inside.

No matter what sort of house you live in, you can always add a little something barefoot to it. Elisa and Michael did just that with their house in Bethesda, Maryland. They discovered the joys of modern architecture only after they'd bought a neocolonial house. The house was still under construction, so

# barefoot out back

they had a chance to eliminate a lot of moldings and curlicues, giving the interior a more contemporary character. But they held off building a porch; and as a result, the house faced its sunny backyard without a satisfying connection. What the house needed, Elisa realized, was a screened porch off the kitchen.

The porch is simply a screen-covered box made from treated-pine framing and cedar slats, louvers, and floor planks. The thoughtful composition of the slats and louvers and the play of light and shadow all create barefoot character.

**The pavilion-like screened porch has an exuberant roof of orange canvas stretched over a lightweight metal frame. The butterfly roof channels rainwater down a rain chain (at right) to the backyard.**

She and Michael asked architects Rick Schneider and Petros Zouzoulas to design something "fun, modern, and colorful."

Rick and Petros studied the backyard, considered the difficulties of adding a modern porch to a traditionally styled house, and came up with a refreshingly barefoot solution: to pull the porch away from the house as a stand-alone pavilion.

## Breaking away

The advantages of a stand-alone porch are many. At a little distance from the colonial house, the porch can express itself as a pure sculptural element, a garden gazebo. Pulled away from the house, it doesn't block light to the kitchen. The space between the house and the porch becomes a deck, introducing a second outdoor space to the backyard. With four screened walls and a screened ceiling beneath its fabric roof, the detached porch allows for ample ventilation, a huge plus in this often muggy Washington, D.C., suburb. And because the porch stands at the far side of the deck, it brings the couple and their children just that much deeper into the yard.

## Degrees of exposure

Each screened wall of the cube-like porch responds to the backyard with a different combination of slats, louvers, and openings, depending on how much privacy, shade, or view is desired. The sides facing

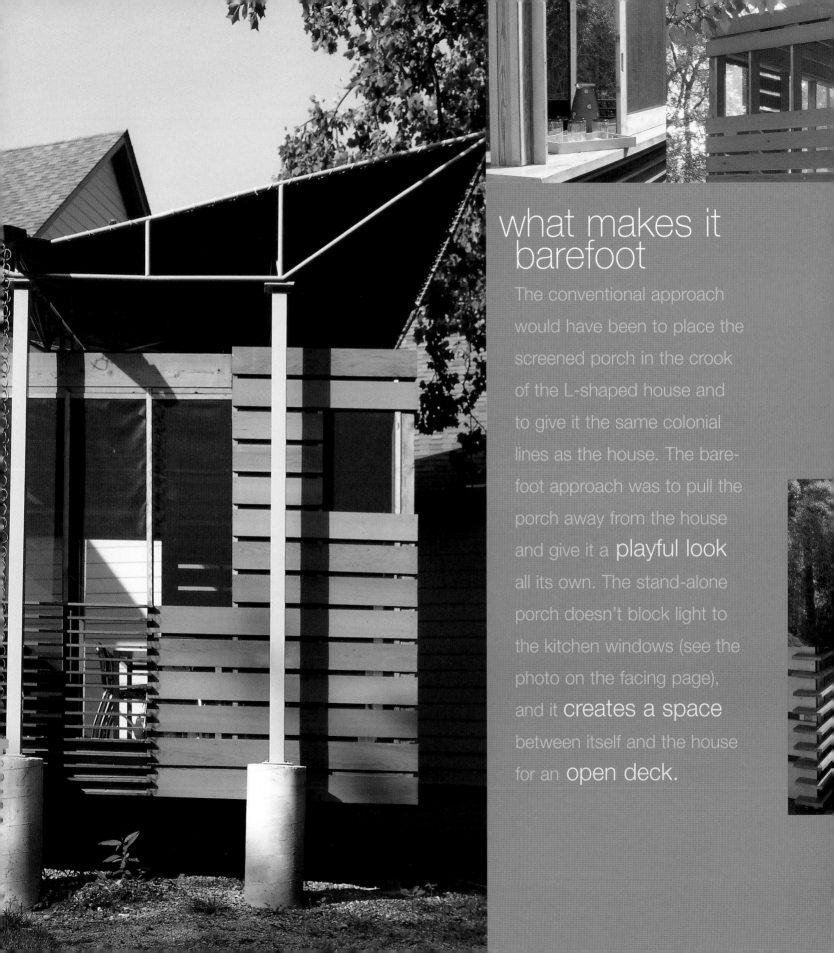

## what makes it barefoot

The conventional approach would have been to place the screened porch in the crook of the L-shaped house and to give it the same colonial lines as the house. The barefoot approach was to pull the porch away from the house and give it a **playful look** all its own. The stand-alone porch doesn't block light to the kitchen windows (see the photo on the facing page), and it **creates a space** between itself and the house for an **open deck.**

# barefoot spirit

"The porch was a chance to do something fun
and modern without having to commit the whole house."

— *Elisa*

the neighbors and the garage wall have wide slats with narrow spaces between them. The sides facing the kitchen and garden have thin louvers with wide spaces between them. A pass-through counter with a sliding screen window makes it easy to ferry food from the kitchen or to stand in the porch and serve guests on the deck. The counter gives the porch the look of a festive lemonade stand.

## A roof alights

The lightweight fabric roof is supported by a delicate metal frame and four thin posts, all entirely independent of the porch cube itself. The inverted roof floats over the porch like a butterfly about to alight, adding real barefoot drama to the backyard.

By day, the porch is a clubhouse for the kids, a quiet spot for lazing away a summer afternoon. By night, its orange roof lit from below, the porch serves its simple purpose with flair, keeping the bugs out and bringing the family together.

On the side facing the kitchen and garden (photo left), the porch opens up with a pass-through counter and thin louvers, which let in more light and allow more view than the flat slats used on the sides facing the neighbors and the garage (photo top left). A butterfly roof suspended above the porch provides shade and keeps out the rain while encouraging ventilation through the screened ceiling.

To reach the detached screened porch, you have to step outside; but once inside again,
you're in a little world apart from the house, poised delightfully over the backyard.

In the hills southeast of Oakland, California, there's a house that's barefoot twice. Barefoot because of its laid-back sensibility and barefoot in the relaxed way it has evolved over time. The house began life in the 1920s as a starter-cottage package deal; for a couple hundred bucks, the original owner got the

# growing barefoot over time

lot, the plans, and a pile of lumber. In the 1970s, a bohemian sculptor added a studio to the back of the cottage, just 440 sq. ft., but generously proportioned and two stories high to catch the light. The sculptor reused an old gym floor, installed salvaged windows (no two alike), and cobbled together long

The main living space connects to the backyard by degrees: Clerestory windows let in garden light; French doors offer easy access; and the alcove thrusts outward, putting you right under the backyard sycamore trees.

# barefoot spirit

"Work with what you've been given. Improvise. It opens up new ideas."

— *Bill*

French doors have a way of beckoning you outside. It must be that the double swing of the doors implies motion, even when one or both doors are shut.

▷ The tiny loft addition feels like a tree house within the main living space. It provides a perch for a small home office while adding scale and visual drama to a space that would feel too tall and empty without it.

roof beams and homemade skylights. The current owners, architect Bill Mastin and his wife, Susan, call the eclectic mix they inherited in the 1980s "hippie carpentry at its best." As Susan and Bill shaped and reshaped the house to suit their needs, they stayed true to the sculptor's spirit of carefree improvisation. The result is a comfortable, highly livable house that's finely tuned to its owners.

## The life of the house shifts to the garden

When Susan and Bill first occupied the house, they lived within the confines of the original cottage, which consisted of a living room, kitchen, bath, and bedroom, all crammed into 525 sq. ft. Susan used the big studio for her photography, Bill for his architectural work. But when they weren't working, the studio cut them off from the backyard, where they'd planted a delightful kitchen garden with herbs, vegetables, berries, and a lemon tree.

They found themselves bringing meals out to the studio to eat, to be closer to the garden and the evening light. So they resolved to turn the studio into a living/dining area, making this two-story space the barefoot center of the house, and to add a kitchen directly off the living space. Susan and Bill turned

In this unfussy house, the stairs borrow the hearthstone as a landing on their way up to the loft. The gas fireplace is raised so it can be seen from the kitchen.

the original living room into a bedroom and the other original rooms into studio spaces. In effect, they flip-flopped the house, putting the private spaces up front and the public spaces in the back.

## A playful approach to remodeling

When he's working on other people's houses, Bill endeavors to think everything through, to coordinate things, to get it all just right. But with his own house, he was forced to meet the casual terms set by the

The dominant form of the two-story main living space holds together an eclectic mix of structures: the bowed-roof alcove, the French doors with their little shed roof, and the kitchen addition (at right).

## what makes it barefoot

The house is an **energetic jumble** of parts pieced together over time, yet you can't miss the main entry, signaled by its roof overhang and purple door. When the main house shifted from the original cottage to the two-story living space and kitchen addition, the front door migrated toward the back, as well. The route inside is now a little longer, but it's a **pleasant walk** through a side yard garden and onto an entry deck built around a plum tree that grew alongside the old house.

sculptor. Instead of tearing it all down and doing it his way, Bill embraced what he found. Much of what the sculptor built made sense—the skylights, for instance, and the clerestory windows—so Bill left it alone. When he did make changes, he did so playfully, experimenting in true barefoot spirit with colors, details, and ideas, sometimes designing on the fly, doing some of the carpentry himself.

The new kitchen, painted a cheery blue and purple, features tilted glass blocks for countertop light, a vintage stove, and a backsplash shaped like a mountain range. The new loft hangs from the beams like a tree house, with splayed sides that play against the quirky angles of the roof. Susan and Bill's approach to furnishing is equally playful. The dining table has wheels, so it can be moved out of the way for dancing; striped curtains take the place of cabinet doors; Susan's photo collages are pinned up without fanfare and moved around often; and the cord to the dining table lamp swoops down from the ceiling in a lazy arc.

◁ **The kitchen has the form and integrity of a proper Greek temple but doesn't take itself too seriously. Its symmetry is relaxed, its colors are playful, and its materials are nothing fancy. Cast-off lengths of wavy-grained fir form a mountain-range backsplash.**

**Windows line up to allow a view from the entry through the kitchen and out to the backyard studio, strengthening the connection between rooms and from inside to out.**

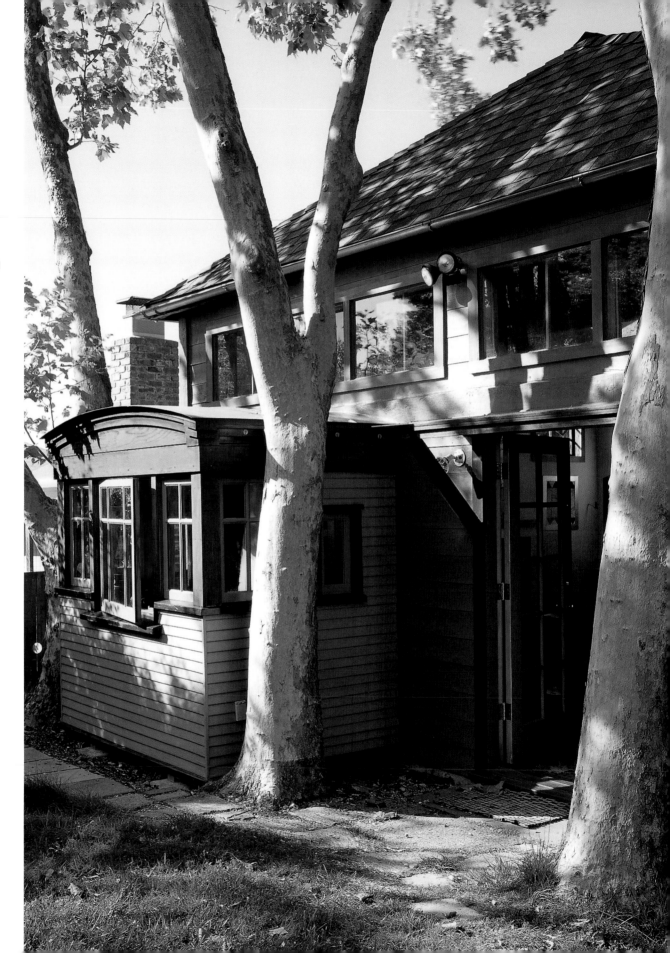

Three huge sycamores are an integral part of the house. You see their leaves through the sky-lights, brush up against them on your way to the garden, and feel the cool of their dappled shade.

# Barefoot cozy

Barefootedness equals openness, it's true, which is why barefoot homes nearly always have a large, open, living space like Susan and Bill's. But barefootedness also allows for intimacy; and for that, there's Bill's alcove addition, just 6 ft. by 6 ft. and a little over 6 ft. tall. It's the first thing that catches your eye when you step into the house.

When you're in the alcove, reading or painting or having a drink, you feel cozy and contained, the way kids do inside a cardboard refrigerator box; but you also feel curiously set free. There are windows on three sides, and you're right up against them; as in a gazebo, you feel the garden all around you. But what's most liberating is that the alcove's there at all. There it is, right off the most important room in the house, the kind of fairy-tale hideaway most of us dream about but forget to build.

The dining alcove juts ever so slightly into the two-story main living space, like a gypsy wagon crashed into the house. A step up from the main floor and intimately detailed, the alcove is a cozy place apart, though it's just an arm's length away.

## footprint

The entire original house (shaded area) is now a private bedroom and studio space. The main living space, entered by skirting around the old house, opens up to the backyard garden. To one side of the main space, the kitchen affords views to the street and entry area as well as to the backyard.

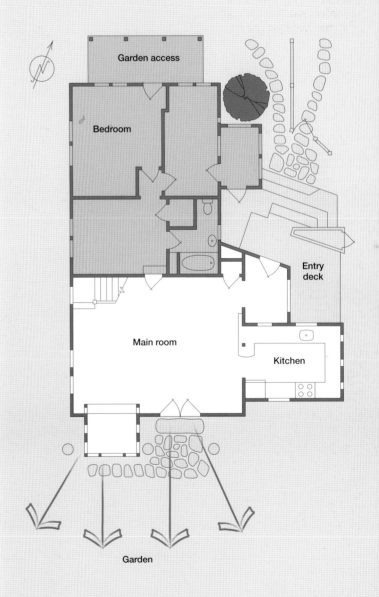

Garden access

Bedroom

Entry deck

Main room

Kitchen

Garden

Openness, informality, a connection to the outdoors . . . these barefoot ideals make sense no matter where you live. How these ideals express themselves, however, is bound to change from place to place. A beach in southern California will suggest one thing, a Kansas prairie quite another. It isn't hard

# barefoot on the prairie

to imagine what a barefoot home in Malibu might look like—stucco walls, tiled roof, glass doors opened to a sandy courtyard shaded by palm trees —but what about a barefoot home on a swale overlooking agricultural bottomland in Douglas County, Kansas? Dan Rockhill didn't think in barefoot terms,

A breezeway frames the landscape between the garage and the house, capturing it for quick study or long, leisurely viewing over a cup of coffee or a glass of beer.

Hinting at the traditional Native American longhouse, the house lies low under its sod roof, blending with the prairie landscape. It's tucked below a swale for protection from the north winds but is open to the sweeping bottomland below it to the south.

A quiet presence on the land, this barefoot Kansas home engages its prairie landscape by bearing witness to it: facing the sun, hearing the howl of the wind, and letting the grasses grow.

but he essentially had them in mind when he set out to design and build a house on spec outside the university town of Lawrence. Wisely, he let the land and its history tell him what to do. What evolved was a long, low house that looks and feels a lot like the simple farm buildings dotting the area.

The place proved perfect for a screenwriter and filmmaker named Jon, who had grown up in Kansas, moved to Los Angeles, and felt the pull to return home. Jon took one look at the shell of the house and realized he was looking at a something rare: A big-city loft placed deftly on the high plains. "This," he said, "is where I want to live."

The honesty and economy of the interior contribute to the home's easy informality. The kitchen is a tidy mix of birch cabinets, stainless-steel appointments, and handmade concrete countertops.

## footprint

This house follows the simple logic of the land, stretching itself east to west so that every room faces the sun and views to the south. A row of tall cabinets runs along the back wall, providing tons of storage and insulating the rooms from the cold north. Similarly, the garage protects the main living space from the intense rays of the setting sun. The interior is open and flexible. The two bedrooms within the core of the house open to the hallways with pivoting panels and can be combined to form one workspace.

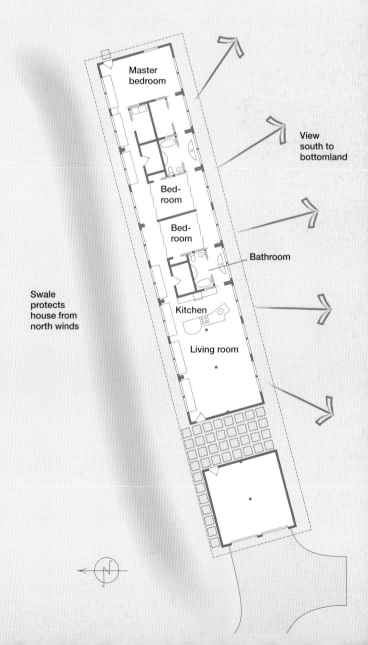

Master bedroom

View south to bottomland

Bed-room

Bed-room

Bathroom

Swale protects house from north winds

Kitchen

Living room

N

# barefoot spirit

"It's incredible to be here in a thunderstorm. I can watch it rolling in, lightning flashing from three sides."

— *Jon*

Though the lowered ceiling above the bed offers a sense of shelter, spending a night in the master bedroom feels like camping on the open prairie, especially when the morning sun pours in.

## Fitted to the land

Now when Jon comes home, he turns off the highway and heads down a long drive through a field of brome grass. As the sound of the highway fades, the house emerges, its sod roof rising up from the farmland, followed by the long, north-facing limestone wall. Jon glimpses a swatch of rich farmland through the breezeway connecting house and garage, and then he's upon it, acres and acres of land stretching southward toward the distant trees.

To the north, the house hunkers down under its sod roof, tucked below the hillside to escape the winter winds. The limestone slabs covering the rear wall hint at the original homestead house, still standing nearby, which was built with local limestone quarried by German immigrants. The slabs require no maintenance and have a solidity and durability equal to the intensity of the Midwestern weather. To the south, the house opens up to the sun and the view through a 12-ft.-tall wall of windows. The windows are protected by a roof overhang and horizontal metal louvers (known to architects as *bris soleil*) that block the high summer sun but allow the low winter sun to reach deep into the interior.

The long, narrow house encourages cross-ventilation. The main rooms—a master bedroom at

The open interior is bright and airy under the tentlike sweep of the high ceiling. The ceiling cants up to high windows on both sides, while the floor flows past the utility spaces and bedrooms that form a solid core at the center of the house.

With clear birch wall panels and cabinetry, a polished concrete floor, and a white-painted drywall ceiling, the interior feels as simple and serene as the prairie.

the east end and a combined living, dining, kitchen area at the west end—are the full depth of the house. Between them is a core of bathrooms, utility spaces, and additional bedrooms with a corridor to either side. The rear corridor is lined with tall, IKEA® cabinets that provide storage and protection from the cold north wall. The front corridor runs alongside the window wall, never relinquishing the view.

# Watching the clouds go by

Walking up and down the length of the house, Jon stays in tune with the horizontal sweep of the land. Kansas isn't an easy place for outdoor living, but Jon will sit in the breezeway from time to time. He uses the rooms in the core of the house for editing, and while the film spools along, the world unfolds all around him. He wakes up to a new sun, sees wild turkeys or spots a coyote up on the ridge. The sun traces a path across the infinite sky. Clouds roll by, an afternoon thunderstorm explodes overhead. The sky clears, night falls, stars come out. The day is a movie, and from his barefoot Kansas longhouse, Jon plays a part in it.

**The twin corridors are anything but dark and dreary. High windows above birch-faced IKEA cabinets bathe the north corridor in soft light (photo top left), while pivoting panel doors open the inner rooms to both hallways. The ballerina-like doors pirouette into the south corridor (photo left).**

## what makes it barefoot

The entire house opens to the south, **providing views** of the farmland beyond. Though the view is grand, it's also entirely private. No curtains are necessary. Two vanity sinks are propped like painter's easels in front of the **south-facing windows.** The bathrooms behind the vanities offer the requisite privacy, but what a thrill to stand in the **open corridor** and freshen up where you can see **deer grazing,** and they can see you right back.

Piazzas, or public plazas, are a big reason why old Italian towns are so charming and livable. A piazza provides a communal, open space for everyone—a place for coming together, a gathering point. One of the simplest but most powerful barefoot ideas is to think of your main living space, especially a com-

# living room as town square

bined living/dining/kitchen area, as a piazza or plaza, as a town square. Architect Nick Noyes had a town square in mind when he helped Richard and Lloyd turn a modest suburban ranch in Santa Barbara into a delightful barefoot home for themselves and their young daughter. Keeping within the original

A house chopped into small rooms makes no sense for a casual, close-knit family, so three rooms were opened into one big space where the family spends a lot of time together.

It's remarkable how bright and open this tiny kitchen feels simply because small windows have been placed between the countertop and cabinets.

Throughout the house, rooms are lightly furnished and casually adorned. Case in point: The travel map collage lining the wall to the master bedroom.

footprint of the house, Nick opened up three rooms to create an airy, loftlike family commons: living room flowing into dining room flowing into kitchen. What makes this open living space so remarkable—and so barefoot—are what Nick calls escape valves: many routes out of the big room into smaller, more private spaces, as well as many connections to the outdoors.

## Lots of openings let the main space breathe

Just as a public square connects to the rest of town through streets and avenues radiating from it, so the main living space here opens outward. The three French doors along the south wall unite the indoor space to a large terrace and to a glimpse of the Pacific Ocean far beyond. A French door at the east end leads to a second terrace at the back, and a door from the kitchen connects straight out to a narrow side yard. There's a short, light-filled hall that leads to the master bedroom; a barn door that slides open to the daughter's room; and, perhaps most important of all, a glassed-in passageway linking the main space with a guest room and home office addition.

An 8-ft.-tall wall of storefront glass connects the guest room (in the foreground) and home office to an intimate backyard terrace. The concrete floor inside flows effortlessly into the concrete paving on the terrace, strengthening the indoor–outdoor connection.

# footprint

The main living space of this modest single-story ranch connects to all four sides of the house through numerous doors. Two terraces and a narrow side yard are just a step away. Most of the doors are tall, outward-swinging French doors whose double-wide openings help blur the distinction between indoors and out. Doors on opposite walls line up with each other, encouraging cross-breezes and creating a sense of flow.

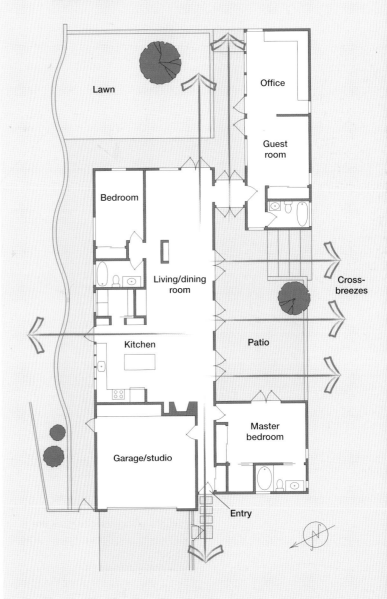

# barefoot spirit

"I get a sense of space all around me, even though it's a small house."

— *Richard*

The lines of this remodeled ranch are clean and spare, yet the feeling inside is open and warm. Easy-to-maintain stucco, aluminum, and concrete make for carefree living.

This wide-open space, with its many glass doors and openings, is airy, informal, and romantic; but there's also a practical reason to it. Although Richard and Lloyd's daughter is a good sleeper, the wall between the main room and her room has two thicknesses of drywall for added sound dampening. Of course, it helps that the family likes to spend time together—that's the true secret to living happily in one big room.

## Light and air are everything

Richard and Lloyd weren't after a town square when they moved from Brooklyn to Santa Barbara. What they wanted was the buoyant quality of light and air they'd experienced years before on the Pacific Coast south of Santa Barbara in Ojai. Realizing this, Nick did one simple thing: He cranked up the south side of the original roof to form a shed roof that sweeps up to the light. Because the ceiling rises to 12 ft., there's room above the French doors for transom windows. The tall ceiling reminds Richard and Lloyd of their converted loft back in Brooklyn, so it feels like home. But here, French doors and transom windows connect them to the whole outdoors.

## what makes it barefoot

If there's one key to the bare-footedness of this remodeled ranch, it's the 6-ft.-long, **glassed-in passageway** between the addition and the original house. Walking through the passageway, even with the glass doors closed, feels like stepping outside and then back inside again. The walkway also defines terraces on either side of it by filling in what would otherwise be an entirely open corner. The little passageway is **both there and not there,** and this small measure of ambiguity makes all the difference.

The glassed-in passageway is the linchpin, connecting the original house (left) to the addition (right), and the side terrace (foreground) to the back terrace (background)

## A house shaped to embrace the outdoors

The original ranch felt like it had been plunked down on the site willy-nilly, with no thought to sun or views or the shape of the property. Now the house embraces the yard in a more meaningful way by dividing it into two terraces. Partly this is the result of a happy accident. At first, the addition was going to be a tower with guest room below, home office above. When that proved unfeasible, Nick, in effect, laid the tower down on its side, so that both the guest room and the home office open onto the back terrace.

The house and the terraces now form a kind of checkerboard of inside and outside. Because the long, thin house and its addition tic-tac across the site, every room has light from two sides and connects to more than one outdoor space. Lloyd feels it when she wakes up in the morning and walks out to the terrace for a cup of coffee. Richard feels it when his feet are propped up on the desk in his office, doors wide open. Their daughter and her friends know it best, perhaps, when they run through and around the house—inside, outside, inside, outside until there's no difference.

The wide opening at the far end of the main living space reveals the home office/guest room addition beyond the terrace. The addition is reached through a glassed-in passageway (to the right of the photo), heightening the interplay of inside and outside.

▷ The 8-ft.-tall, all-glass French doors expand the main living space out to the sunny, south-facing side terrace. Passion flower vines spilling down from a trellis above the doors soften the opening and echo the green landscape beyond.

Some barefoot homes blend so seamlessly with their surroundings you hardly notice them. But a house doesn't have to be camouflaged to be barefoot. The house Dan built for his wife, Debbie, and their two young children in the Sierra foothills east of Sacramento, California, makes no bones about

## slice of life

being an object in the landscape. Dan and Debbie's house is a tall, thin sliver, just 12 ft. wide, a sculptural wedge that slices into the sky like a rock promontory growing from the hill. Its connection to the landscape comes not from how it hugs the ground but from how it juts into the view, says architect

The rock-walled terrace provides a generous outdoor space for family dining or large gatherings. The wooden deck beyond offers a dramatic spot for taking in the view.

Though the loft was designed as a children's play space, it also makes a dramatic perch for a bed, an ideal spot for kicking back and taking in the morning sun.

The house responds to its hillside site by expanding upward and outward, capturing a distant view and making the sun, the sky, and the stars a part of everyday life.

Paul Almond, who designed the house with his partner, Pam Whitehead. "The house doesn't cheat you out of the experience of the hillside."

# Freedom of form

"The forest, in a sense, is simply interrupted by the house," Paul says, commenting on the skinny shape of the house. Because it was designed to be a guest house, the total area is under 1,200 sq. ft. In addition, Dan and Debbie had a long wish list. They wanted light, openness, and two stories to capture the view. They wanted communal space as well as private space. They wanted to build green and be energy efficient. They wanted the warmth of wood but not the heaviness. It's a lot to ask of a little house. And it all had to be buildable by Dan, who would be learning on the job.

The easygoing modernism Paul and Pam embrace gave them freedom to play with the form of the house in response to Dan and Debbie's many requirements as well as in response to the land. The resulting wedge-shaped house is contained and cozy at the back (perfect for private bedrooms) and soaring and open at the front, just right for the communal living room and the loft above. Constructing the narrow, upswept house called for honest framework—long beams, angled roof supports, and exposed ceiling joists, but not for intricate joinery or heavy timbers. Dan was ready to rise to the challenge.

## what makes it barefoot

Two 6-ft.-wide, 8-ft.-tall glass **doors slide away** from the corner of the living room, allowing the indoor space to continue onto the deck. The **cable railings** on the deck offer a secure measure of containment while maintaining the impression that the living room and the deck are **floating like a ship** above the distant hills.

# barefoot spirit
"The forest, in a sense, is simply interrupted by the house."
— *Paul Almond, architect*

## A house shaped for drama

From back to front (north to south), the character of the house changes dramatically. The master bedroom, sunken a few feet into the ground, feels like a warm cocoon. Next comes the kitchen, an in-between space, which is grounded yet draws light from the living room. The living room is washed in light from tall windows rising on three sides, although the partial ceiling formed by the loft above shelters the space and keeps it from feeling overexposed. Springing out from the living room, the front deck floats above the trees like the prow of a ship. Standing on it gives you an exhilarated, almost jittery feeling.

The shape of the house is also the secret to its energy efficiency, especially during the long, hot summer months, when cool air enters the ground-level windows to the north, sweeps through the house, and rises up and out. The pronounced roof overhang protects the south-facing windows from the high summer sun, and the lattice wall of the outdoor staircase blocks the late-afternoon sun to the west.

**Open shelves lend the small kitchen a relaxed, everything's-at-arm's-reach feel. The low shelves between the kitchen and the living room allow light, conversation, and heat from the woodstove to flow freely.**

Soaring windows give the house a feeling of expansiveness well beyond its 1,200 sq. ft., an acknowledgment that on a hillside the sky is as important as the ground.

# footprint

The house roots itself in the hillside to the north, where cozy bedrooms nestle between thick walls, then juts out from the hill toward the south, expanding to capture a big view. Because the house is just 12 ft. wide, the hillside seems to flow through it from side to side.

Open to the view

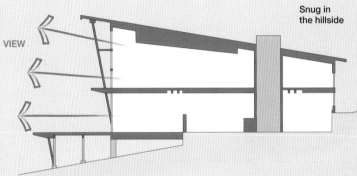

VIEW

Snug in the hillside

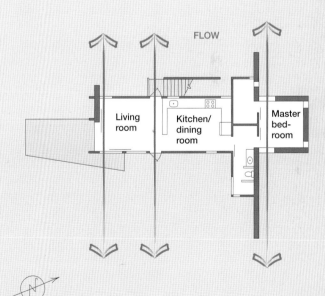

FLOW

Living room

Kitchen/ dining room

Master bed- room

# An active home for an active family

The outdoor staircase is one of the most barefoot aspects of the house. Paul and Pam suggested putting the stairs outside to save precious square footage inside. Dan and Debbie liked the idea of stepping out to come in again, so much so they even said no to an indoor ship's ladder. This is a family that spends as much time as possible in the various outdoor spaces surrounding their razor-thin house: enjoying lunch on the shaded patio to the north, tucked between the house and the hill; dining on the terraced patio to the east, the sun comfortably blocked by the house; or simply sitting and talking on the jutting deck, watching a hawk go by. The kids' favorite outdoor space is the cave-like nook under the deck and living room, which encapsulates the yin–yang of the whole house, offering, at once, a sense of shelter and a feeling of great expansiveness.

An outdoor staircase turns the act of going upstairs and downstairs into a barefoot stroll. As the only set of stairs, an outdoor staircase isn't for everyone, but it's a welcome option on warm and sunny days.

With its mottled slate tiles and heated concrete floor, the bath is snug and earthy; in pleasant contrast, the corner windows, tilted toward the sun, hint at the airy expanse outside.

▷ Standing in the loft, about to head out to the short balcony above the entry door, you feel suspended in midair, as though you were in a tree house. Being able to see through the floor joists to the living room below heightens the effect.

Texture gets short shrift in our homes. We talk easily about light and space: "This room is bright, that room is large"; about orientation: "This room faces south, that room faces east"; even about circulation: "There's a good flow between these rooms." But we rarely speak of how our homes

## a feel for natural materials

feel to the touch. That's too bad, because the tactile qualities of materials and surfaces can have a tremendous impact on our experience of home. Texture is especially important in a barefoot home, where the feel of things contributes immeasurably to our sense of informality.

The natural materials in this sunroom—roughsawn wood, stucco, and painted wood—combine with soft colors and warm sunlight to create a richly textured, yet relaxed ambiance.

The old farmhouse (to the left) and the addition (to the right) fit together as naturally as the combined house sits in the Virginia countryside.

The doorway between the family room and the covered deck offers a nifty answer to the question of how to screen a large opening. Here, screen doors hang from tracks on the outside of the transom and glass doors hang from tracks on the inside.

Texture is in many respects the dominant theme of Charlie and Wendy's barefoot farmhouse in the foothills of Virginia's Blue Ridge Mountains. When Charlie got in touch with architect Alan Dynerman to help renovate the old house, one of the first things he told Alan was that he didn't want any drywall. Charlie thought back on his childhood home in Connecticut, with its pebbled stucco walls and rugged whitewashed stonework in the basement. By contrast, Charlie felt drywall looked too new and crisp, too smooth, too temporary. He wanted his farmhouse to have the settled-in quality of his boyhood home. Accordingly, Alan employed a palette of simple, rough, natural materials—oak plank flooring, fieldstone, roughhewn beams, troweled stucco—all rich in rustic texture and barefoot informality.

# Knitting together old and new

In place of a one-story addition from the 1950s, Alan designed a sympathetic, stucco-clad addition to the century-old clapboard-sided house. The addition is anchored at one end by a sunroom with a master bedroom suite above it. With its own gabled roof, this wing of the addition looks almost like a small house. Instead of opening up the original house, Alan turned it into bedrooms for Charlie and Wendy's four grown boys. A large family room and a sweeping kitchen connect the new master bedroom wing to the old house. The combined family room and

## what makes it barefoot

The unassuming, informal entry area presents a rich mix of **rustic textures:** a peeled cedar column, a tumbled-stone floor, a field-stone step, roughhewn oak beams, painted wood ceiling boards, **stucco walls,** oak stairs. If you haven't begun to relax as your foot falls on the **tumbled stones** upon entering, you will by the time you brush past the **peeled cedar** column.

# barefoot spirit

"I love the feeling of solidity you get from stucco and stone."

— *Charlie*

The south-facing exterior wall of the breakfast nook strikes a balance between openness and enclosure. The stucco, stone, and wood offer a sense of shelter, while floor-to-ceiling glass lets space and light flow.

▷ The breakfast nook is a quiet, casual spot a few steps below the kitchen, where you can sip tea and read the paper and contemplate the day unfolding outside.

kitchen—Charlie calls it the "big room"—is now the heart of the house.

The house rises and falls with the land. There are steps between the old porch and the new deck; steps spilling down the deck to the yard; steps from the family room up into the old house; steps down from the kitchen into the breakfast nook; and two full staircases, one leading up to the master bedroom and one leading up to the boys' bedrooms.

The kitchen is an easygoing galley with a hard-wearing floor of softly rounded fieldstones, thickly painted wood cabinets, and soapstone countertops that gain a patina with age. It's not too slick or precious for whipping up a rustic meal.

Extending the roof of the old porch over the new deck ties the original farmhouse to the addition. The porch is partially enclosed by posts and railings, whereas the deck is more open, so there's a variety of outdoor space under the roof.

◁ The big fieldstone chimney and shallow Rumford fireplace, which puts the fire almost into the room, are the very essence of the hearth, a place for pulling up a chair and warming your feet.

With the big glass doors rolled back, the covered deck and family room take on the feel of an open-air pavilion, connected by light, openings, and views to both sides of the house.

With its mix of gentle colors, the bedroom is as laid-back as the surrounding foothills. Throw open the French doors, and a cool mountain breeze comes in with the morning sun.

Negotiating the steps—some made of stone, some of oak—slows Charlie and Wendy down just a little and literally puts them in touch with the house.

# An easy mix of color, light, and texture

As Charlie and Wendy go about the house, they brush past the peeled cedar post by the stairs, they glide across the tumbled stone floor in the kitchen, they feel the cracks between the oak plank floorboards. They experience not only the richness of the textures but the interplay of rough, natural materials with bold paint colors and dramatic sunlight.

The story-and-a-half family room is lit not only from its east-facing wall of glass but also from west-facing clerestory windows above the heavy ceiling beam separating it from the kitchen. The high clerestory windows allow light deep into the room, where it washes the roughhewn roof framing above and falls gently on the wide, oak flooring planks, the exquisitely laid field-stone hearth, and two pale yellow side walls—one of stucco, one of wood. The pale yellow walls are set off by colonial blue trim, and the whole room gets a jolt from the rich purple-blue and red of the cabinets and counters that stand between the family room and the kitchen. There's a lot going on, but the mix of colors, textures, and light is pulled off with such balance and restraint that the effect is as calming as the rolling pastureland that cradles the house.

## footprint

This remodeled farmhouse is made up of three sections. The original farmhouse has been turned into a guest room and sitting room downstairs and children's bedrooms upstairs. The addition includes a two-story section, with a sunroom below and master bedroom suite above, and a single-story family room and kitchen section. The family room is the hub, connecting the old and new ends of the house, opening to the kitchen and flowing out to the deck and pastureland beyond.

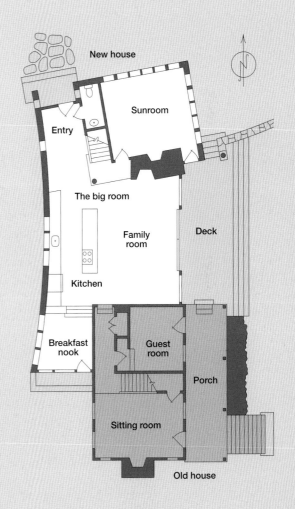

New house

Sunroom

Entry

The big room

Deck

Family room

Kitchen

Breakfast nook

Guest room

Porch

Sitting room

Old house

Searching for a sanctuary in the bustling San Francisco Bay area, John discovered a tiny straw-bale *casita* that had been recently built on the back lot of an older home in Berkeley. Designed by architect Dietmar Lorenz, the little house was quiet, private, and earth friendly—just what John was looking

# barefoot *casita*

for. And because John went in with friends on the purchase (they got the big house; he got the *casita*) his barefoot haven was affordable.

To reach the casita from the street, John enters through a gate in a high wooden fence and strolls past his friends' house along a densely planted

**A doorway nearly as wide as the patio and the living space beyond creates a sense that it's all one big light-filled room. Inside or out, the sun's the same.**

garden path. Bright red curtains hanging from a wooden trellis draw him forward. He steps onto a slate patio and enters through a 2-ft.-thick doorway. John falls into an easy chair, and there are the red curtains again, seen this time through tall French doors that open to the patio. After a day spent working in San Francisco, it's time to unwind in a soft, light-filled space. A compact kitchen and a small dining table are at the far end of the room, and a sitting area surrounds him. Upstairs is a bedroom, a bath, and a desk area beyond the stair landing. That's the whole of John's 850-sq.-ft. home.

## Thick walls, soft lines, peaceful curves

The more time John spends in his living space, the more tranquil he feels. Sunlight falls gently through the translucent panel above the south-facing trellis. A concrete floor the color of a worn penny is cool in the summer, warm in the winter (from hot-water heating pipes embedded in it). There's clarity in the simple dimensions of the room but also a pleasant easing of its lines, the result of plaster troweled over the strawbale walls. At every corner are curves instead of crisp edges. The walls look like they were made of dough, as though they could be reshaped with the push of a hand. John feels safe, secure, and surprisingly secluded, given that there are houses close around—all the result of the thick strawbale walls.

Red canvas curtains hung from cables beneath the trellis can be extended to create an intimate enclosure, but even when drawn back they give the patio the feeling of an outdoor room.

The curved gable-end wall in the bedroom has an imperfect earthiness that's decidedly informal and provides enough depth for a casual window seat. A wall made of stacked strawbales can be finished with straight edges or plastered over in soft curves, as are the sides of this window opening.

◁ The way you arrive at a home can be as barefoot as the home itself. The festive red curtains and the gravel pathway draw you through the loosely planted garden, setting you up for the informality of the little backyard *casita*.

# barefoot spirit

"Open the gate, walk into the property, and you're in a different world."

—*John*

Walls made from stacks of strawbales—held together with wire mesh, then covered in concrete outside and plaster inside—make the cottage energy-efficient. The walls hold in heat or keep it out, helping the house maintain an even temperature without requiring much energy. But more than that, the thick, earthen walls give the little house barefoot character John can literally reach out and touch.

## In the company of sunlight

Sunlight is a frequent visitor, a companion for John over the course of the day. And in a home furnished as simply as this one, the play of light is all the more pronounced. Early morning light reaches the east-facing bedroom and study windows; late morning light pours into the living space; afternoon light spills down the stairs from the greenhouse windows. In winter, the low sun reaches clear across the living space to the kitchen. As the sunlight changes in tenor across the hours and seasons, so do the plaster walls, shifting through shades of yellow and orange. It's sunlight, after all, that illuminates and animates the curves, and it's the curves that make John smile.

The stairway is flooded with light from a greenhouse window above. Moving between floors beneath the greenhouse glass feels like stepping outside under the trees and coming back in again.

## what makes it barefoot

Though the living room is not large, the doorway connecting it to the patio is **generously proportioned.** Because the ceiling is 9 ft. high, the doors can be 8 ft. tall and still have a narrow transom window above them. The concrete living-room floor is level with the slate patio, further **connecting indoors to out.** Red curtains hanging both within and without add still more indoor–outdoor impact.

Many of us have fond memories or cherished dreams of summers at the beach. Of long, barefoot days, sparkling ocean waves, warm sand between our toes. If our memories or dreams conjure up a house, it's as often as not a simple, spare cottage, modestly furnished, uninsulated, with wall

a simple summerhouse

studs and rafters exposed—a place that's utterly, purposely, happily unfit for winter . . . the barest of barefoot homes. Even if our interest lies in a year-round home somewhere other than the beach, a summerhouse on the ocean is a fitting barefoot paradigm. Noel and Ellen had such a place on

The cottage sits quietly behind the dunes, with its corrugated concrete roof, weathered cedar shingles, and muted colors in tune with the rugged beauty of the windswept beach.

This simple summer cottage lets the ocean tell it how to be: tucked behind the dunes for protection from the wind and rising tides, yet perched high enough to capture sea breezes and a big view.

The way the ocean mists and salt air turn everything gray is something to celebrate, not something to worry about. Materials like these cedar posts and steel re-bar railings were selected because they look good when weathered.

Fire Island—the long, thin barrier island south of Long Island, New York—and now they have another. Their first place was a local landmark of 1950s funk, a contemporary cottage with just one main room, two small bedrooms, and a bath. The cottage looked enough like a food shack that people would come off the beach onto the oceanfront deck looking for hot dogs. Noel and Ellen loved the cottage and tried desperately to keep it, but it was too worn out to save.

To rebuild, the couple called architect Fred Stelle. They wanted more space than in their old cottage, but the same barefoot feeling. They showed Fred images of Japanese pavilions and Thai houses on

Of the cottage's three pavilions, the one closest to the beach—the main living pavilion—is the smallest, minimizing its visual impact while maximizing its intimacy with the waterfront.

stilts, and Fred blended these with images of summer cottages in Maine and on Cape Cod. The resulting cottage is made up of three connected pavilions on stilts. Though this cottage is the largest barefoot home in this book, it is, in many ways, the simplest.

# A deliberate lack of refinement

Fred thought of the three cottage pavilions as little more than unadorned plywood boxes. The spaces are carefully planned, but they look casual. Indeed, the exposed framing and honest details make the interior look just built.

## footprint

The cottage is shaped like a pinwheel, with a main living pavilion overlooking the ocean and two bedroom pavilions stepped back to create pockets of more private outdoor space. The sitting and dining areas in the main living pavilion have wide ocean views and easy connections to the waterfront deck, but they're also the most exposed to the sun, wind, and water. The bedrooms capture the sound of the waves and plenty of sunlight while offering more personal views of the water.

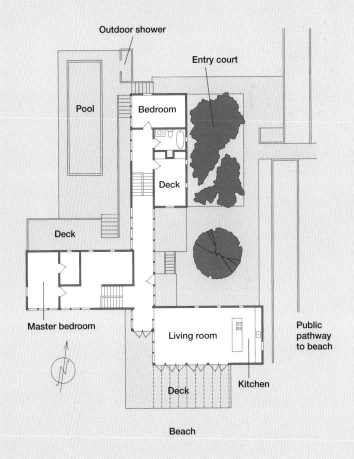

Outdoor shower

Entry court

Pool

Bedroom

Deck

Deck

Master bedroom

Living room

Public pathway to beach

Kitchen

Deck

Beach

# barefoot spirit

"Despite its size, this is really just a shed on the beach."

— *Ellen*

The sun bathes the softly bleached plywood walls with the same ethereal light that falls on the beach, casting a serene spell over the stair hall and bedrooms.

The interior materials appear natural, almost as though they came from the beach outside. The wall studs, ceiling joists, rafters, and plywood sheathing are lightly stained to the bleached gray color of driftwood. The polished bamboo floors are the pale amber of the dune grasses in autumn.

The stairs are simply bamboo planks on open stringers, and the stair railings are steel re-bar and cables. Galvanized aluminum lighting fixtures hang from the ceiling rafters with visible bolts, and the conduit that runs electricity to the lights and the

From the south end of the entry hall, you can head straight out to the front deck or turn left into the main living space. Either way, you get the ocean.

A generous hallway puts some space between the parents' quarters (to the left) and the children's quarters (far end of hall). The hall is brightened up with simple materials: lightly stained plywood, exposed rafters, open stairs, and cedar shingles.

switch plates is also visible. Everything is durable, basic, and decidedly low-key. This deliberate lack of refinement puts the house in the background, where it fosters a deep sense of serenity.

# A quiet retreat from a noisy world

Noel and Ellen's Fire Island beach community matches the informality and simplicity of their cottage. Their long-settled town is laid out on a Lilliputian grid

The homeowners never check the ferry schedule. "When we get here, we get here" is their laid-back approach. After all, the waves are eternal.

The walls in the bath are clad in the same cement boards used on the exterior fascias, not to make the bath feel like it's outdoors but because plainness and durability make as much sense inside as out.

# what makes it barefoot

The main living space, seen here at the kitchen end, is bare-bones shelter. **Exposed framing,** plain shelving and cabinetry, and re-bar tie rods stretching between the rafters give the space the feeling of having just been built. This deliberate **lack of refinement** recalls summer cottages of old, but the true reason to build this sparely is the same as the reason to be at the beach in the first place: to **relax,** peel away the worries, and get **down to the essence** of things.

In the quiet of a back bedroom, there's nothing to distract you from listening to the sound of the waves or losing yourself in a good book.

of walking paths that works its calming magic as Noel and Ellen stroll from the ferry dock to their house, and the cottage needs only to maintain the effect.

What Noel and Ellen want is some quiet in a busy world; and for that, they need very little. "How can you relax," Ellen asks, "if you're looking at tons of stuff?" Instead of "looking at stuff," she looks out at the ocean or simply listens to it, lying in bed at night with the windows open and the lights out. The ocean is a presence here, a tangible force, and yet it also stretches out beyond the horizon and beyond the imagination. That's why it's so endlessly fascinating to sit in a simple summerhouse by the ocean and look, listen, and wonder.

▷ The most heavily used spot in the house is nothing more than a sofa, two chairs, and a coffee table at one end of the main living space. No carpet, no lamps, no hearth, no fanfare of any kind. What matters is the ocean and the open space, inside and out.

Imagine you're standing on a smooth, flat rock somewhere high in the mountains. It's a summer morning, the rock faces east, and you're barefoot. The sun has been up for an hour, and in that time, it's begun to warm the rock, though the air is still slightly cool. The sunlight dances

## the warmth of
## sun and earth

on your feet, and its warmth seeps into your skin. You know you've got to get moving, but you linger just a little longer, and then a little longer still.

This is what it feels like to wake up in the small, adobe guesthouse built by architect Bill Hoffmann

The house faces east, where the rising sun lingers low on the horizon, its long, penetrating rays inviting visitors to start the day, perhaps with a cup of tea in the dining room.

Even with a storm approaching, the earthen walls of this adobe casita light up with the sun, the easy curves and softened edges offering guests a warm welcome no matter what the passing clouds might bring.

A gravel pathway curving through a high-desert cottage garden connects the main house to the laid-back guesthouse, where it's okay if a little gravel comes in with the guests.

and his wife, Georgia, in Taos, New Mexico, where the sun shines through the clear, high-altitude air 320 days a year. Bill and Georgia built the casita close to their own adobe home to encourage visits from their grown children and Georgia's new granddaughter. They call the little house Casa de las Abuelas, or "House of the Grandmothers," because they built it with a friend of Georgia's, also a new grandmother. All agreed the casita should offer privacy from neighboring houses and blend in with the pueblo-style buildings of the historic town. Georgia wanted the same barefoot elements she insisted on in the main house: sun and light in every room, no narrow corridors, and a window seat for reading in the afternoon.

There's a quiet barefoot simplicity to the forms and surfaces of this bedroom vignette: the arch of the doorway echoed in the curve of the little niche, the plainness of the sandstone floor and plaster wall giving light a place to linger.

The courtyard is as much an extension of the interior of the house as it is its own outdoor living space. The trellis-covered *ramada* is, in turn, a room within the courtyard, offering welcome shade from the afternoon and evening sun.

# Courtyard connection

To take full advantage of the sunny weather, Bill shaped the house around a courtyard situated to the southeast of the house. Each of the main rooms—living room, dining room, and bedroom—opens onto the courtyard through generous French doors. The living and dining rooms face east, so they receive direct sunlight across the morning; the bedroom faces south, drawing morning light in winter but not in summer, when visiting family members are likely to want to sleep in. The house itself blocks the intense western sun, shading much of the courtyard from the afternoon heat. At the same time, the wall separating the courtyard from the surrounding garden is far enough east of the house to capture the delightful hues of sunsets, where they can be enjoyed from the shade, under the trellis-covered *ramada*.

The floors throughout the interior are covered in split-face sandstone, a rugged earth-toned material that stands up to kids, dogs, and people coming and going from the courtyard and garden. Just as important, the sandstone pavers continue out into the courtyard, where they form a patio, tying the indoor spaces to the courtyard, not just visually but texturally. Walking barefoot in the house *feels* exactly the same as walking barefoot in the courtyard.

Split-face sandstone tiles that echo the hard earth of the Southwest flow smoothly from the courtyard through the doorway to the bedroom, connecting outside to inside, the house to the land.

# what makes it barefoot

Guests who stay in Casa de las Abuelas (House of the Grandmothers), respond naturally to the soft curves of its **sculpted adobe walls.** The 10-in.-thick walls are made by stacking individual mud bricks, each a **sunbaked mixture** of clay, sand, and soil with straw, water, and a little asphalt. The bricks are then covered with plaster. The resulting walls are **earthy, honest,** and delightfully barefoot. Visiting grandchildren have no trouble kicking off their shoes and **getting relaxed.**

# barefoot spirit

"It's difficult to be pretentious about detail or formal in your lifestyle when your walls are made of mud."

— *Bill*

The arched opening puts a little psychic distance between the expansiveness of the garden and the seclusion of the courtyard. Though it connects outside to outside, the doorway implies movement from room to room.

## A liquid flow of space

Although the house is just 1,275 sq. ft., it feels spacious. In part this is because it opens out to the courtyard. But Bill also used a couple of visual tricks to make the interior seem larger than it is. One was to establish diagonal views, such as the long stretch between the far corners of the living room and dining room (as shown in the photo on the facing page). Another was to layer space by only partially separating the rooms, so it's possible to see from one space through a second space and into a third, as you can from the living room, through the foyer, and into the sleeping alcove (see the photo on p. 177). These are small spaces, and yet taken together, they feel quite expansive.

The sense of flow from one space to the next is heightened further by the materials Bill used. The undulating adobe walls don't suggest a firm beginning or ending to a room but rather an easing from one space to another. Through these soft openings, the sandstone floor meanders like a quiet stream.

The living room, dining room, and kitchen (behind the stepped wall) are connected enough for casual barefoot conversation to flow between them, yet divided enough to provide a measure of privacy necessary in a small house.

◁ The sculptural curves of the hearth and traditional stepped adobe wall, called a *padercita*, lend the interior a relaxed softness that invites carefree living. Who could think hard thoughts in such a soft, curvaceous place?

Little is hidden in this barefoot kitchen, where the shelves are open, the appliances are what they are, and the sandstone floor tiles, mud and plaster walls, and round roof beams express their true nature.

# Naturally barefoot

The sandstone floors are a pleasure to walk on, cool in the summer, warm in the morning sun, heated in winter by hot-water tubes embedded beneath them. The sandstone is cut into large slabs but it isn't polished or finely worked. It looks and feels like the earth. From the floors to the walls and ceilings, the primary materials of the house are natural (Bill calls them "God-made"), and they're used in their most primitive and original forms: thick timbers for lintels above the windows; round logs, called *vigas,* as roof beams; sun-dried adobe bricks for the walls. The adobe is sculpted in rounded and sensual shapes and smoothed over with gypsum plaster inside and cement plaster outside. More than anything else, it's the imperfect curves of the adobe that promote informality. As Bill puts it, "It's difficult to be pretentious about detail or formal in your lifestyle when your walls are made of mud."

# footprint

The way this little house wraps around an enclosed courtyard provides both privacy from neighbors and openness to the outdoors. Because of the L-shaped floor plan and the angle of the dining room, it's possible to be inside looking out through the courtyard and back into the house. Large French doors allow space to flow from the main rooms to the courtyard, just as space flows easily from room to room through large openings in the thick adobe walls.

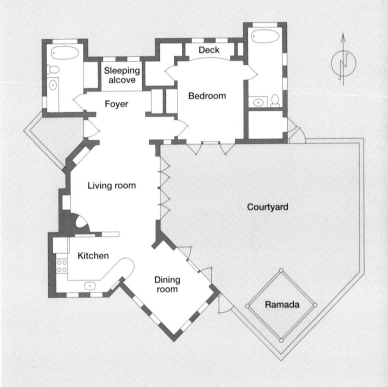

A few years ago, architect John Jennings and landscape architect Sasha Tarnopolsky bought a Spanish Colonial Revival house in suburban Los Angeles with a derelict garage behind it. They saw the garage as a barefoot opportunity. Thinking outside the box, they tore down the 400-sq.-ft. building

# barefoot garage

and put up a 640-sq.-ft. mini-house in its place. The mini-house consists of one room with a sleeping loft plus a bath separated by a short, covered walkway. The foundation was already there, and the mini-house is small and simply made, so it is inexpensive space. John and Sasha call the new building a

**This backyard mini-house stands on the footprint of a former garage. It serves as guest quarters, home office, auxiliary storage, laundry area, and play space.**

In place of a tumbledown garage stands a mini-house that provides guest quarters, studio space, play space, and storage while bringing the backyard to life. Its cool stucco walls are the perfect backdrop for a garden patio under an olive tree.

The no-frills laundry area doubles as a small kitchen, allowing the mini-house to be used as full-time living quarters.

There's no pretending in this laid-back, one-room living space. Everything is what it is, from the plywood cabinets to the two wall-mounted heating units, stripped of their beige plastic coverings.

studio, but it's really a catch-all auxiliary to their 1,100-sq.-ft. home. It's also an inviting backdrop to a serene backyard garden.

# Garage as mini-house

For the next two years, John and Sasha lived in the mini-house while they renovated the main house. Now the mini-house is where John's parents stay during the three months they visit each year. It's also a play space for John and Sasha's two children, with art supplies at the ready; it's a laundry room, with the washer and dryer for the house; it's storage space for bikes and surfboards; it's an extra bath, with an outdoor shower behind it that drains into a bed of bamboo; it's a home office; and it's a TV room. The mini-house takes up slack so there's more room in

A ladder climbs one side of a built-in bookcase, leading the way to a nestlike loft suspended from the rafters. Clerestory windows throw light into the loft and down into the kitchen/laundry area.

# barefoot spirit

"Outdoor space is very important to us. The whole property is our house."

—*Sasha*

In place of the old driveway, a garden path of concrete squares and grass links the mini-house to the main house.

the main house for the family. Sure, it's easy to live this way in southern California, but even here, the mini-house represents fresh thinking. Visitors step inside, expecting a garage, and their eyes open wide: "You mean you can do *this*?"

## A reason to go outside

Having a detached mini-house means having to go outside, sometimes for basic things like laundry, but it also means making the most of the whole yard. Where the driveway once was, John and Sasha now have a garden with vegetables, fruit trees, and a fish pond. The space between the house and the garage has become a patio area under an olive tree. The couple likes having to walk through the garden to get to the only TV; it keeps things in perspective. Building codes require the mini-house to function as a garage if need be (hence, the concrete floor and the big doors), so John and Sasha could take the TV out and put the cars in. But why would anyone want to do a thing like that?

## what makes it barefoot

The informality of this back-yard living space owes a lot to a **paired-down palette** of a few basic materials—Douglas fir framing (**much of it recycled** from the old garage), plywood, and Homasote® fiberboard (the gray panels between the wall studs)—all finished plainly with a mixture of **beeswax** and linseed oil.

Colette and Kelly had a couple of things in mind when they set out to build a summer home for themselves and their four children on a small island in Puget Sound near Seattle. Colette had fond memories of summers spent on the island in her family's vacation home, which was not a conventional cottage but

## stay-at-home
## summer camp

a modern house designed by a Chicago architect. It was a bright, open place with big, wide windows and lots of decks, and it gave Colette an appreciation for the simplicity and clean lines of modern design. But she and Kelly wanted something a little

A big reason the kitchen feels so easygoing is that it opens directly onto this side porch, a sunny, little spot for a sip of coffee or a quick dose of fresh ocean air.

Instead of plugging into the TV, the children can slide open the barn door to their art room and paint out in the garden.

The outdoor shower is nothing fancy, just a little plumbing under the eaves, a quiet place to wash off and warm up before ducking around the corner and going in through the side porch.

more barefoot, a home with the openness and honesty of a modern house but not the sleek styling.

Above all, Colette and Kelly wanted an alternative to their traditional home in suburban Chicago. As they told their architect, Rex Hohlbein, they didn't want a "typical drywall house." What they wanted was a relaxed, low-maintenance barefoot home that would encourage rough-and-tumble summertime family living.

## Adopting a child's point-of-view

The idea behind the house was to give the children new experiences and fresh ways of looking at things, a feeling of having been to summer camp. To get at a primal barefootedness that sometimes eludes grown-ups, Rex imagined the house from the children's perspective. He put the emphasis on the porches, especially the wide front porch, and on the family space on the first floor, whichis really just a big kitchen (making pancakes) that's open to a living room (playing board games) and an art room (painting stepping-stones for the garden). There's no TV in the house, no individual bedrooms for the kids, not even a quiet getaway room—though there is a window seat that's perfect for reading a book. The point is for the kids to hang out together, mostly outside.

All four kids share one bedroom, with a panel that slides down the middle when a little privacy is needed. But they often abandon the room in favor of

The work area between the kitchen islands is the hub of the house, connected in one direction to the living room and the ocean view, in the other to the children's art room, with enough space to either side for people to hang out without getting in the way.

# barefoot spirit

"We always eat outside, on the front porch, looking out toward the water."

— *Colette*

The south porch is many things: an entry stoop, an outdoor hearth where dinners are cooked on a grill that fits the firebox, and a rooftop sleeping deck the kids reach by climbing out the bathroom window, sleeping bags and pillows in hand.

the concrete-floored roof deck above the entry porch (see the photo above). At night, the kids and perhaps a cousin or two climb through the master-bathroom window with their pillows and sleeping bags and spread out under the stars. The air cools off on most nights, but the concrete deck still holds the warmth of the day. It's a delightful barefoot combination.

## what makes it barefoot

As materials go, plywood is honest, durable, easy to care for, and utterly **without pretense.** In this summer-house, the ceiling and walls are surfaced with sheets of ordinary plywood given a clear finish to bring out an **amber glow.** Plywood is also used for the kitchen cabinets, whose doors and drawer fronts have finger holes in place of knobs . . . the epitome of barefoot casual. Plywood is **warm and subdued,** a perfect backdrop to the life of the family, which, after all, is what really matters.

This bare-bones hearth is made from board-formed concrete. The tall Rumford fireplace, its back wall blackened with use, lets you see the tips of the flames, just like a campfire.

The generously proportioned waterfront porch functions as an extension of the living room and as an outdoor room in its own right, with space enough for dining, napping, and summertime projects.

▷ The house is quite small for a couple, four children, and frequent gatherings of extended family and friends, but the big sliding doors extend the open interior onto the porch and out to the yard.

# Keeping it simple

Besides giving the kids the run of the house, Colette and Kelly wanted to entertain lots of extended family and friends. And they wanted the house to be open to the outdoors, the outdoors being the reason for spending summers on the island in the first place. But they also enjoy cozying up to the fire with a cup of coffee in the quiet of a cool morning. They wanted barefoot openness, but with the possibility for intimacy.

Rex responded to this twin desire by keeping everything simple. The simple form of the pitched roof sheds Pacific Northwest rains and provides a sense of shelter, especially to the bedrooms within the roof itself. The simple, boxlike main spaces—each connected to the other, each with a door to the outside—are open enough to handle large gatherings, yet small enough individually to feel comfortable with just a few people in them.

But it's the simple materials, inside and out, that really give this house its barefoot character. Cedar siding, open ship's ladder-like stairs, board-formed concrete . . . each contributes to the kids' camplike experience. The Rumford fireplace, its tall and shallow firebox characteristically blackened with soot, puts a campfire right in the living room. It's an indoor fire reduced to it simplest form.

Simplest of all, though, is the primary surface material on the inside of the house: not drywall or plaster but plain old plywood, albeit selected for

Perched above a narrow stretch of Puget Sound, the house doesn't draw attention to itself but instead provides a variety of spots—porches, roof deck, and window seat—where one can relax and enjoy the outdoors.

To enter the house from the driveway, visitors curve left around the garden and slip in a side porch . . . the barefoot opposite of a grand staircase and formal entry hall.

good grain and a minimum of football-shaped plugs. Colette and Kelly were skeptical of plywood at first, but now they love its warm, amber glow, the perfect complement to the rich green landscape beyond every door and window.

# Barefoot moment

There's a time late in the day when the setting sun angles through the west-facing front porch and bathes the plywood in golden light. Colette and Kelly might be inside to catch it, but more likely they're lingering at the table on the front porch, looking out at the distant Olympic Mountains in silhouette. The house is to their backs, and it hardly matters whether the walls are plywood or plaster. The kids are circling the house, zipping by much faster than the sun. It's all about the barefoot moment.

## footprint

This floor plan is a good example of barefoot minimalism. At the core are four spaces arranged in a line toward an ocean view: art room, kitchen, living room, and front porch. Each connects directly to the outdoors. The more functional entry porches, laundry room, and bath (as well as the window seat, stairs, and hearth) are placed along the sides of the main spaces, where they don't interrupt the view or the feeling of openness.

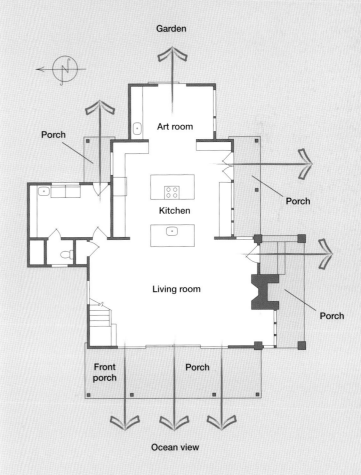

Whether you're building a new house or remodeling an old one, every choice you make during design and construction can make your home more barefoot. If you choose a big room for everyday living instead of a separate kitchen, dining room, and living room, your home will likely be more barefoot.

# barefoot by choice

Choose exposed wood ceiling beams instead of drywall-covered ceilings, and you'll nudge your home in a barefoot direction. Even little things can make a difference: open shelving in the kitchen instead of cabinets, glass doors instead of solid ones . . . each of these adds barefoot character.

A sandy path leads to a welcoming entryway and a south-facing deck that's protected by the L-shaped house from winds coming off the water. Even before reaching the glass doors, you see clear through the house to the dunes beyond.

There are hallways and then there are barefoot hallways. This example of the latter feels bright and open thanks to a high ceiling, striped flooring, and a long row of windows.

# As different from normal as possible

When architect Jo Landefeld set out to design a getaway home on the Oregon coast for her husband, John, and their two young daughters, she decided to make it "as different from a normal house as possible." She wanted a barefoot cottage by the sea, not a place that felt like their city home. Jo recalled summer cottages she'd rented on Fire Island, back East. They weren't winterized, and often they had exposed wall framing—no drywall, no paneling, no nothing—just 2×4 studs, with the horizontal blocking between the studs serving as impromptu shelves. The Fire Island cottages had outdoor showers, lots of windows, and decks with built-in benches where everyone spent their time. What mattered was the beach. The honest interiors and outdoor focus of the Fire Island cottages became Jo's guiding vision.

Despite weather that's often cold and damp, Jo insisted on exposing the wall and roof framing (and

Though a slight change in the heights of the countertops and windowsills provides a subtle shift from the kitchen area to the dining area, everything from cooking to eating to kids' art projects happens in one big room that opens onto a deck.

## footprint

The open living space of this Oregon-coast home fronts beach dunes and a path to the ocean, where the action is. The living space and the long bedroom wing form an L-shape that protects the south-facing deck from strong winds, making it a safe haven for sunning and the all-important nightly barbecue. The north deck extends the living space out toward the dunes, and the small deck to the east provides a place for washing off sand or taking an outdoor shower.

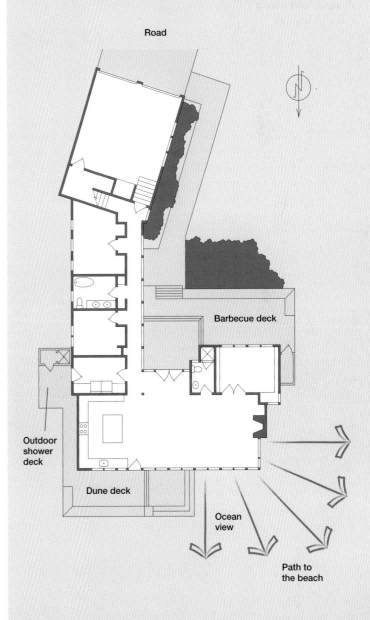

Road

Barbecue deck

Outdoor
shower
deck

Dune deck

Ocean
view

Path to
the beach

# barefoot spirit

"When you're inside the house, you're really outside.
You're always at the beach."

— *Jo*

In this barefoot beach house, the structure (wall posts, roof beams, steel tie-rods) is the decoration. There's only the wall above the mantel for artwork; but who cares when the whole living space opens out to sand dunes and ocean?

placing insulation panels to the outside). "There's something comforting," she says, "about seeing what holds up the roof." Accordingly, the shape and structure of the spaces in the Oregon house are more important than the finishes, which are plain and simple. Wood roof trusses with steel tie-rods, wood posts supporting the trusses, rough-sawn roof planks . . . these define the spaces more than wall coverings or paint or artwork. In a similar vein, the plentiful windows are simply glass panels set between the posts, with little or no trim around them. In this barefoot cottage, after all, the interior spaces take a back seat to the outdoor decks and the grass-covered dunes.

## Barefoot economics

Jo and John wanted a place for relaxing and enjoying life outdoors, not a second home to labor over. They also had a budget. And so, without ever calling it by name, Jo practiced barefoot economics. Letting the house's simple structure be its decoration was the first step toward affordable barefoot living. The second step was choosing materials for their cost, durability, and ease of maintenance.

The decking is a composite material made from wood fiber and plastic; it doesn't quite have the

## what makes it barefoot

The sweeping corner window seat, which seems to pull the **sand dunes** right into the living space, is both connected to the larger space and sheltered under the low soffit. Besides **adding intimacy,** the soffit houses recessed downlights for reading as well as uplights for illuminating the ceiling above. Mismatched denim blue cushions and baskets for children's toys fit the **bare-bones aesthetic** of the interior, which is, in turn, an echo of the spare coastal landscape just outside.

The master bedroom (below) is a small room, but it feels airy and open thanks to exposed ceiling beams, a bevy of windows, and a glass door to a private a balcony (right).

silvery patina of cedar, but it costs less, lasts longer, requires minimal care, and—best of all—won't give splinters to barefoot kids. The windows are vinyl rather than wood for the same reason. But the exterior siding is the real deal: cedar shingles—expensive, but renowned for their longevity. Almost as important, the rich, natural texture of the cedar shingles and trim counters the plastic smoothness of the vinyl windows.

To complement the natural fir framing inside, Jo chose plain, inexpensive materials. The kitchen countertops are plastic laminate, about as unfussy as you can get. The floors throughout are covered with linoleum tiles laid in a striped pattern. The colors of the linoleum stripes, beige and light brown, were picked to hide all the sand that gets tracked in.

The natural fir framing, cabinetry, and shelving form a neutral backdrop for the playful colors and simple forms of everyday objects. In this honest, open, informal home, things are what they are, whether bowls, chairs, lamps, or roof beams.

# Free to boogie board and barbecue

There's a discipline to designing a simple house and an effort involved in choosing the right materials, but the payoff is carefree barefoot living. With the house able to fend for itself, Jo and John can turn their attention to seabirds and wildlife, and the kids can don wet suits, grab their Boogie® boards, and head for the waves. When big storms roll in, the family gathers inside and enjoys the spectacle, warmed by the radiant-heated floors. And virtually every night, John barbecues dinner on the sheltered, south-facing deck. The grill is so important it's stored in the little shedlike addition you see clipped to the house in photo on the facing page. Giving the barbecue grill its own room . . . now that's a barefoot decision.

The wide-open entry area tells you right off that you've stepped into a barefoot home. You're greeted by a floor of light, rough slate tiles, and no fussy closet— just coat hooks.

The beach is joined to the house by a cedar plank pathway through tall dune grasses. The long wall of windows opens to the ocean view and to comings and goings along the path.

The daybed on the stair landing makes a fine place for a young guest to sleep, but even when just the family is around, it's a reminder, often heeded, to relax and enjoy the view.

Openness. A lack of clutter. The two ideas are not exactly the same, but in a barefoot home, they often go hand in hand. Boston real estate developer Dave understood this intuitively when he decided to pare down and simplify his life. He took a few months off work and went on a road trip across the country,

# uncluttered home,
## uncluttered life

looking for ideas about the kind of house he wanted but mostly just chilling out. When he came back to New England, he bought a run-down cottage on Peaks Island, which sits in Casco Bay, three miles from Portland, Maine. He moved to the cottage and

Here's how to turn a cramped cottage into a bright, airy barefoot home: Blow out the walls, cut a hole in the ceiling, fill a gable full of windows, and refashion the interior with birch plywood, sandblasted glass, and ground steel that glints in the light.

The steel mesh that gives the interior much of its barefoot panache is a clever sandwich of two perforated screens, one with little holes, one with bigger ones, a combination that lets through a little light and view, but not too much.

found a new, less-stressful job in Portland. He went from wearing a suit and tie in the big city to pulling on a pair of jeans and ambling down to the ferry in the morning for a 15-minute boat ride to town. When Dave called architect Will Winkelman to remodel his home, he was ready to make his cottage as uncomplicated as his life.

## Cottage on the outside, loft on the inside

The existing cottage was cramped and confused, a funky rabbit's warren of tiny spaces, bedrooms barely 7 ft. wide, and a living room at the center completely cut off from light and air. "It was totally inboard," Will says, putting it in suitably nautical terms. The good news was that the shell of the cottage was well built and worth keeping. Will and Dave began by replacing the windows, doors, and siding and by adding more windows for light and views, all without knowing exactly how they'd change the interior.

But there was never any question they'd open up the inside as much as possible, nudging the little cottage toward the light and airy feeling of a loft. Dave was satisfied with two bedrooms under the eaves instead of the original three, which freed up the space between and gave Will the idea to cut a hole in the floor and let light from the newly glazed southern gable end spill downstairs. Will also shifted the location of the stairs, setting them at a rakish angle to add dynamic energy and allow the back of the house to become one big light-filled living space.

◁ **The freshly clad and painted cottage projects a sunny disposition but only hints at its open interior. It's as fit for its traditional neighborhood as it is for barefoot living.**

## footprint

The difference between the original cottage floor plan, with its warren of cramped rooms, and the new floor plan, with its open living space, is the difference between a buttoned-up home and a barefoot one. Take note of the dotted line on the new floor plan: It represents the opening in the ceiling that lets sunlight in from above—and that really changes everything.

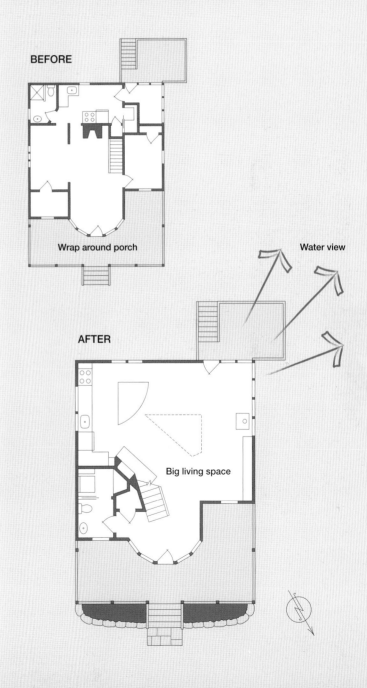

BEFORE

Wrap around porch

AFTER

Water view

Big living space

In place of the maze of walls that cut up the old interior and starved it of light, a dynamic composition of angled glass, steel columns, and curved mesh livens up the new interior while maintaining its bright, open feel.

The sunny southeast corner of the open living space is the sweet spot, bringing together the warmth of a wood-stove with a glimpse of the water, plus a full look back at the entire, light-filled interior.

## A new world order...beginning with the stairs

Dave worked right alongside builder Jim Peletier until the transformation of the interior was complete. Now as you enter the house from the front porch, you experience the stairs as a sculptural element within a tall space, which expands toward the far southwest corner of the house, where there's a narrow water view. The stairs angle in line with the view, and this new orientation is reinforced even more strongly by a grid of plywood floor panels.

As tight and efficient as a ship's galley, the kitchen epitomizes the simple, open, uncluttered feel of the remodeled cottage. It's an unfussy space for turning out an unhurried meal.

# barefoot spirit

"This house is an expression of me after I decided
to slow down and unclutter my life."

—*Dave*

**Putting a skylight over the bathtub
was an impromptu decision, made
during remodeling, but it makes all the
difference to this small space tucked
under the eaves.**

The remodeled interior is an entirely different cottage from what you'd expect from the outside—a roomy, comfortable place that perfectly fits Dave's streamlined life. The big space has discrete spots for cooking, dining, listening to music, reading by the fire, and working at a desk; and yet it doesn't feel cramped or crowded. Partly that's because Dave keeps it free of tchotchkes and knickknacks, but mostly it's because Will and Dave stuck to a limited palette of clean, barefoot materials: blond birch, sandblasted glass, and plain ground steel.

## A yellow glow

Dave has always been drawn to loft spaces because they're clean, spare, and full of light. Funny thing is, when he worked in Boston, he lived in a basement apartment. Now that he's on a Maine island, he has his loft. It isn't spacious—his bedroom is only slightly larger than a walk-in closet—but it's bright, cozy, and warm. And at night he looks out and sees the stars. By turns, neighbors walking by say Dave's cottage has a yellow glow to it. It's a simple cottage for a simple life.

## what makes it barefoot

If the cottage has a barefoot secret, it's the **wall of windows** that fills the gable end facing south to the backyard. Sunshine comes pouring in, filling the upstairs with **dramatic light** and—more important—spilling down through an opening in the floor to light the living space below. The windows also **draw air up** through the opening, ventilating the whole house on warm days.

# architects and designers

## Letting the Light In

Tom Bosworth, FAIA
Bosworth Hoedemaker
1408 North 45th Street
Seattle, WA 98103
206.545.8434
www.bosworthhoedemaker.com

## Alfresco Oasis in the City

Rod E. Novion, AIA
Novion Group, Inc.
3316 Northeast 125th Street
Seattle, WA 98125
206.361.6133

## House and Garden Are One

Robert Edson Swain, AIA
Robert Edson Swain, Inc.
member Edge, LLC.
5339 Ballard Avenue NW
Seattle, WA 98107
206.784.4822, Ext. 102
www.bobswain.com

## Barefoot Cubed

Charles Rose Architects, Inc.
formerly Thompson and Rose
Architects, Inc.
115 Willow Avenue
Somerville, MA 02144
617.628.5033
www.charlesrosearchitects.com

## Barefoot under a Big Roof

Brad Burke
Brad Burke, Architect
PO Box 1514
Poway, CA 92074
858.513.0824
www.bradburkearchitect.com

## Building Upward and Outward

Taal Safdie and Ricardo Rabines
Safdie Rabines Architects
1101 Washington Place
San Diego, CA 92103
619.297.6153
www.safdierabines.com

## Opening Up in New England

James Estes, FAIA
Estes/Twombly Architects, Inc.
79 Thames Street
Newport, RI 02840
401.846.3336
www.estestwombly.com

## Open to the Breeze

Taylor Dawson III, AIA
Taylor Dawson & Associates
310 21st Street N
Suite 100A
Birmingham, AL 35203
205.328.4455
http://www.taylordawson.com

## A Plan for Coming Together

Anni Tilt and David Arkin, AIA
Arkin Tilt Architects
1101 8th Street, #180
Berkeley, CA 94710
510.528.9830
www.arkintilt.com

## Barefoot on the Prairie

Dan Rockhill
Rockhill and Associates
1546 East 350 Road
Lecompton, KS 66050
785.393.0747
www.rockhillandassociates.com

## Farmhouse on the Beach

Bob Hull, FAIA and Scott Wolf, AIA
The Miller Hull Partnership
Polson Building
71 Columbia, 6th Floor
Seattle, WA 98104
206.682.6837
www.millerhull.com

## Living Room as Town Square

Nick Noyes
Nick Noyes Architecture
2325 Third Street, Suite 341
San Francisco, CA 94107
415.512.9234
www.nnarchitecture.com

## Barefoot Out Back

Rick Harlan Schneider, AIA,
and Petros Zouzoulas
Inscape Studio
1215 Connecticut Avenue NW
3rd Floor
Washington, DC 20036
202.416.0333
www.inscapestudio.com

## Slice of Life

Paul Almond, AIA,
and Pam Whitehead, AIA
Sage Architecture, Inc.
2400 22nd St., Suite 220
Sacramento, CA 95818
916.456.3553
www.sagearchitecture.com

## Growing Barefoot over Time

Bill Mastin, Architect
6633 Mokelumne Avenue
Oakland, CA 94605
510.562.4004

## A Feel for Natural Materials

Alan Dynerman
Dynerman Whitesell Architects
1025 33rd Street NW
Washington, DC 20007
202.337.1290
www.dwarchitects.com

# architects and designers

## Barefoot *Casita*

Dietmar Lorenz
DSA Architects
1107 Virginia Street
Berkeley, CA 94702
510.526.1935
www.dsaarch.com

## Stay-at-Home Summer Camp

Rex Hohlbein, Matt Waddington
Rex Hohlbein Architects
18116 101st Avenue NE
Bothell, WA 98011
425.487.3655
www.rexhohlbeinarchitects.com

## A Simple Summerhouse

Fred Stelle, AIA
StelleArchitects
48 Foster Avenue
PO Box 3002
Bridgehampton, NY 11932
631.537.0019
www.stelleco.com

## Barefoot by Choice

Jo Landefeld Architect
3145 Northeast 21st Avenue
Portland, OR 97212
503.222.3010

## The Warmth of Sun and Earth

Daniel W. Hoffmann, AIA
DWH Architects
PO Box 1157
Taos, NM 87571
505.751.1479
www.dwhoffmann.com

## Uncluttered Home, Uncluttered Life

Will Winkelman, AIA
Whitten + Winkelman, Architects
37 Silver Street
Portland, ME 04101
207.774.0111
www.ww-architects.com

## Barefoot Garage

John Jennings and
Sasha Tarnopolsky
DRY Design, Inc.
5727 Venice Boulevard
Los Angeles, CA 90019
323.954.9084
www.drydesign.com

KIRKWOOD

2-31-07

728
VASSALLO

Vassallo, Marc
Barefoot home

KIRKWOOD

Atlanta-Fulton Public Library